LORENNE M.G. CLARK is a member of the Department of Philosophy at the University of Toronto. LYNDA LANGE is a PhD candidate at the University of Toronto. Both have written a number of articles on feminism and philosophy.

In a tradition established by Plato and consistently echoed by later political theorists, woman's role in any social division of labour has been defined by her unique capacity for reproduction. This definition has entailed or justified her relegation to a lesser status – or no status at all – in all other social functions. These essays, written by young academics in philosophy and related disciplines, take issue with an assumption that is now clearly untenable.

The nurture, education, and socialization of children are no longer directly linked to the bearing of children; reproductive labour, in this wider sense, need not be, and in many cases is not, exclusively a female function. Furthermore, productive labour is no longer a predominantly male function.

An introductory essay establishes the theme explored in detail in the later essays. These deal with what might be called the male myopia in the political theories of Plato, Locke, Hume, Rousseau, Hegel, Marx, and Nietzsche. The papers argue that sexist assumptions are so deeply rooted in the western political tradition as to neglect – or preclude – the possibility of equality between the sexes. And if these assumptions are removed, very little is left of the theory.

The volume as a whole will occupy a key place in the proliferating literature of the women's movement. It might lead, as well, to a significant improvement in the thinking of current liberal and Marxist political theorists.

EDITED BY
LORENNE M.G. CLARK
AND
LYNDA LANGE

The Sexism of
Social and Political Theory:
Women and Reproduction
from Plato to Nietzsche

UNIVERSITY OF TORONTO PRESS

Toronto Buffalo London

© University of Toronto Press 1979
Toronto   Buffalo   London
Printed in Canada

Reprinted 1989

Library of Congress Cataloging in Publication Data

Main entry under title:

The Sexism of social and political theory.

Bibliography: p.
1. Sex discrimination against women–History–
Addresses, essays, lectures. 2. Women–History–
Addresses, essays, lectures. I. Clark, Lorenne M. G.
II. Lange, Lynda, 1943-
HQ1122.s39   301.41'2   79-17862
ISBN 0-8020-5459-5
ISBN 0-8020-6375-6 pbk.

This work has been published with the help of
a grant from the Andrew W. Mellon Foundation to
University of Toronto Press.

Contents

TO C.B. MACPHERSON

Introduction

LORENNE M.G. CLARK AND LYNDA LANGE

This collection of essays is meant to raise a new and fundamental question for political philosophy: What would be the effect of assuming that one criterion of the present interest or relevance of any political theory is whether or not sexual equality is a feature of it? We believe that political theory in the past neither made this assumption nor generated theories compatible with it. This resulted from its failure to recognize that the manner of reproduction in human societies requires as thorough an understanding as do other matters with which political philosophy has traditionally been concerned, such as the manner of production or the basis of authority. We contend that traditional political theory is sexist, not merely because women have been deemed to have an inferior nature or social role but, more importantly, because women literally have not been considered 'political animals' in the major theoretical models of political society.

Within these theories reproductive labour has never been assumed to be *social* labour. It is important at the start to define what we mean by 'reproduction' and 'reproductive labour.' Reproduction is the whole process from conception, through birth, to the point of personal independence of the child. It includes the 'reproductive labour' of directly nurturing and socializing children. This labour, unlike other forms of labour essential to the continuation of society, has not been assumed to have any theoretical significance. It is assumed instead to be an aspect of purely personal relationships, and an outgrowth of the natural association of the sexes. Traditional political theory assumes that women bear some unique relation to reproductive labour itself, and not just to the *biological* process, such that it is seen to fall naturally to them to perform it, to the exclusion, at least in theory, of any other form of labour.

Women, *qua women*, are excluded from the public, political, and economic spheres.

The sexism of traditional political theory is thus fundamental, and so long as these assumptions are considered to be merely examples of superficial bias (when they are acknowledged at all), it is inevitable that women should be assumed not to be the equals of men and should be denied rights which would give them both theoretical and practical political equality.

All of the contributors to the present volume share the belief that the sexism apparent in traditional political theory is of this fundamental character, and it is this shared belief which provides that common link in writers otherwise very diverse. Each essay deals directly with one or more of the issues which we believe to be central to an understanding of why traditional political theory is deficient from a feminist point of view. Although the contributors do not all share the same conceptual framework, we believe that their similarities are more important than their differences. Each approaches his or her subject in terms of at least one of the two assumptions which we take to be essential for the creation of a set of sexually egalitarian social and institutional practices. The first is that an adequate political theory must allow the same rights, duties, privileges, and liabilities to all persons regardless of gender. The second is that reproductive labour is as socially necessary and humanly important as productive labour.

An adequate feminist critique of the body of existing theory and the development of a new body of theory free of these deficiencies can only occur if built on firm foundations. We believe it is essential therefore to present the theoretical framework within which we think that questions about women in society, and about the essential task of reproductive labour, ought to be approached. While we cannot resist the temptation, or ignore the challenge, to offer what we believe to be the proper framework within which to carry on such discussions, we do so in the hope that this particular framework will be useful in providing others with a critical theory to use in their own investigations. The volume also includes a bibliography of recent feminist philosophy, for reference and teaching purposes.

We believe that the basic starting point for both a feminist analysis of traditional political theory, and the creation of a substantive feminist political theory, is an analysis of the position of women in the past. Political feminism must begin with a recognition of the inferior status of women both in theory and in practice where these have occurred. But it must go beyond this to analyse the *specific* form and causes of women's inequality. Within traditional political theory the assumed cause of women's inferiority – and of the social inequalities in which this is reflected – is ultimately to be found in biology. Women are alleged to be inferior 'by nature,' and their social inequality is alleged to be a result of their supposed biologically 'disadvantaged' condition. The source of this biological inferiority is said to be the difference in the reproductive capacities of men and women. Since women are the only sex biologically capable of bearing and breast-feeding children, they have been regarded as suffering from a natural liability which creates a natural dependence on males. This is then enshrined in theory in the dependent status created by matrimony, when wives are under the subjugation of their husbands in return for the support which husbands provide for them and for their children. Within this tradition, marriage is regarded as a natural institution which arises independently of political or social organization. It is seen to be a natural outgrowth of the different sexual and reproductive capacities of the sexes, and is therefore taken to be a necessary and inevitable form of association grounded in nature and immune from fundamental change.

On account of these assumptions, many political theories have an ontology which is male. Most theory, up to the nineteenth century, explicitly excluded females. In some theories, terms like 'citizen,' and 'man' or 'men,' are extensionally male, even though they were not necessarily conceived of as excluding women. In the former group are the theories of Aristotle, Rousseau, Hobbes, Locke, and Hegel. Examples of the latter are Bentham and Marx. The theories assume the existence of the family, but the domain of application of the theory is outside the family, and hence does not consider it explicitly. Thus distinctively political institutions exclude the family, and distinctively social – as contrasted with personal – relations are assumed to be those outside the family and to be relations which hold, in theory at least, between males.

While the major theoretical preoccupations of traditional political theory have been the problems of political obligation and authority, these have been thought to be 'problems' only in connection with institutions and relations traditionally regarded as *political*. Since the family has been considered to fall outside the public – political – sphere, the paradigms of justification for political obligation have not been regarded as applying to it. Despite the fact that brute force was a major factor creating obligation and the basis of authority, political theory has been largely preoccupied with attempting to show that authority and obligation are legitimate, genuinely or truly binding, if and only if they are grounded on something other than the power of the sword. The concepts of consent, voluntary agreement, and the social contract were invented as answers to this problem, but they were never seen to be relevant to the institution of the family and the structure of authority within it.

Questions as to the legitimacy and limits of coercion are also questions which have been seen to apply only within the public political sphere and have not been asked about the 'natural' association of the family and the 'personal' relations found within it. The allegedly pre-political, 'natural' character of the authority of men over women and the consequent obligation of wives to obey husbands made justification in terms of the 'main' theory unnecessary. The family has been characterized as the sphere of 'love,' but political theory has had little to say about what rules should come into play when 'love' vanishes.

The first major break with the tradition occurs with Marx and Engels, who argued that traditional political theory was for the most part nothing but window-dressing for the *status quo*. They argued that it obscured the real reasons for social forms being as they were by offering various justifications for inequality, when in fact it was the institution of private property which accounted for the basic structure of social organization. They argued that private property necessarily results in unequal distribution and the division of society into classes with different relations to the means of production, and it is this which is the real material base of social organization.

In our view their criticisms of traditional political theory did not go far enough. They failed to recognize the full theoretical and practical implications of the different status of men and women concerning the ownership of private property. They did not pay sufficient attention to the fact that women and their offspring have been to an overwhelming extent seen as *forms* of private property under the ownership of individual males. Inequality in the distribution of private property between men and women has been and is just as characteristic of society as inequality in the distribution of private property among different classes of men. Marx and Engels simply did not acknowledge the significance of the fact that the system they were concerned with was a system of private property *under virtually exclusive male control* which in fact provided the material base of social and economic structures.

Nothing in the nature of private property itself dictates that available forms of private property should be under virtually exclusive male ownership, or that rights of inheritance should be traced through the male line of descent. But the system of private property which developed into capitalism and its variations was characterized by this principle, and it has been as important in shaping social forms as has been class inequality arising from different relationships to the means of production. Indeed it was the need to maintain a system of private property under primarily male ownership which accounts for the fact that traditional theory assumed reproductive labour was to be a private labour of love and that women were regarded as inferior persons. If reproductive labour had been seen to be as socially necessary as productive labour, then it would have been impossible to argue that it was rightfully done for nothing and it would have been equally impossible to argue that women were rightfully regarded as inferior because of the 'natural' character of the labour they were constrained to perform.

We maintain that the different relation of the sexes to reproduction has had at least as profound an effect on the structure of society as the different relation of individuals to private property arising from production. The nature of this profound effect is found precisely in the fact that this different relationship is not rooted in nature at all, but in convention. It was because the differing sexual relation to reproductive labour was regarded as 'natural' that it was believed to be unnecessary to explain how it came about that women were essentially reproductive rather than productive labourers, and, hence, to show how this fact shaped social organization. Precisely because this difference is in fact conventional we must now re-examine our history to show why the division of labour between the sexes emerged as it did, and how this arrangement served to maintain a system in which both women and reproductive labour were condemned to dependent servility.

We maintain that the different relation of men and women to productive labour in the past is indeed explicable in terms of their differing roles in relation to reproduction. But we maintain that this is in no way a justification of the inequality, since it was precisely by denying women rights of access to remunerated productive labour that they came to have a 'unique' role in relation to reproduction. Reproduction had to be turned into a purely private activity under the exclusive control of individual male heads of households if these latter were to use biological continuity in the preservation of their exclusive right to determine future rights of ownership over their property. The property relation between the sexes became crystallized in the marital and familial relationship, in which women have been subject to varying degrees of authority and control on the part of fathers or husbands. This property relation is thus fundamental to the maintenance of a system of private property which includes the right of inheritance.

To their credit, Marx and Engels recognized that women were oppressed, that is, *unjustifiably* alloted an unequal status. But they ascribed this exclusively to the fact that they lacked access to the productive labour force. Equal access to production is, however, only half the story. Equal liability for reproductive labour is the other half of the story. Marx and Engels were, from a theoretical point of view, almost as remiss as their predecessors in failing to see the necessity for democratization of reproduction as well as of production.

Once this need is recognized, however, it becomes clearer why women, children, and the family were regarded as they were within traditional political theory. The alleged facts of biology and natural inferiority which were used to explain and to justify the fact that women owned no property and were essentially reproductive labourers can be seen to be just as ideological as the alleged natural differences between individual men which were used to explain and to justify the inequality characteristic of class society. Beliefs about the alleged natural differences between individual men supported a society in which some men were disadvantaged not by natural differences in intelligence, industry, or rationality, but through being denied access to ownership and control of the means of production. So also beliefs concerning the inferiority of women supported a sexually unequal society in which women were disadvantaged not by natural differences which made them inferior to men, but through being forcibly restricted to the sphere of reproductive labour. This restriction was itself accomplished by denying them the right to remunerative productive labour, access to ownership and control of the means of production, and the right to determine their sexual and reproductive lives.

What all of the various and appalling philosophies about women amount to in practice is the doing of reproductive labour exclusively by women. All the talk about the limitations of women, such as their lack of 'higher' reason, and other such 'innate' factors, boils down in practice to the idea that women as a group are the ones who ought rightly to perform reproductive labour. The institution of matrimony ensured both that this labour would be performed, and that it would be done by women. Without rights of reproductive control, women had no choice but to bear children, and as the chattels of their husbands, with an exclusively sexual and reproductive function, they lacked these or any other

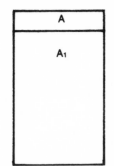

Mental labour or idleness
and ownership of the means of production

Productive labour
and non-ownership of the means of production

Diagram 1

rights the exercise of which would have quickly demonstrated that their abilities and capacities are no less differentially distributed than they are among men. It is our contention that the provision of an egalitarian theory of reproduction is, therefore, the paramount task of contemporary political philosophy.

Our substantive claims about reproduction may be easily understood through the use of a very simple scheme. The function of this elementary model is mainly to enable the reader to clarify the differences between our theoretical perspective and that of others who have also dealt with the problem of 'women's work.'

Political theory has always implicitly recognized the necessity of two kinds of labour, the labour of production, and the labour of reproduction. Indeed, this is enshrined in the fundamentally important concept of the 'division of labour,' which always starts from the alleged 'natural' division of labour between the sexes or within the family. But there has been a general failure to define reproductive labour *as labour* in any politically or economically useful sense, to say nothing of acknowledging that it has been exploited labour. In the history of political theory, the division of labour in society has been seen as shown in diagram 1. Marx was not the first to notice that society depended in a practical way on the efforts of individuals of type A_1. He was, however, the first to be critical of this arrangement in a theoretical way, whereas almost all previous theories had consisted of various attempts to justify it. But a comprehensive view of the division of labour is more like diagram 2.

Political theory has been, as a matter of definition, quite literally about the citizens – *politēs* – sphere A, the male sphere, to the active exclusion

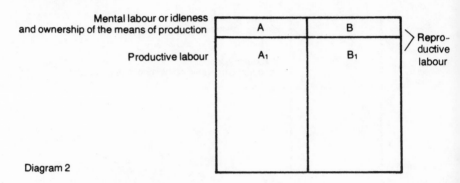

Diagram 2

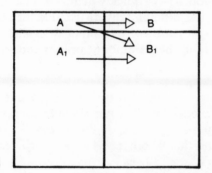

Diagram 3

of sphere B. The activities of these spheres are characterized by many important concepts, all of them with important implicit assumptions. Sphere A is the sphere of 'productive' or 'political' activity, of 'public' life, and the life of reason. Sphere B, that of women, is that of 'non-productive,' 'non-political,' '*merely* reproductive,' 'private,' 'natural,' and emotional activity. We would suggest that all of these concepts are deeply ideological.

There are several important dissimilarities between spheres A and B. For one thing, whereas a minority of males of type A control by means of rule and ownership the vast majority of both the males and females remaining, the control by females of other females is minimal, and control by females of males is virtually non-existent.

Furthermore, for marriage, or for that matter for all heterosexual relationships, the initiative and the subsequent control run in the direction of the arrows (see diagram 3). In most theory women are normally confined to sphere B, and men occupy space in both spheres. In other words, within such a theory a man may be said to have both a public and a private life, whereas a woman may have only a 'private' life. Whether or not a man is in a position to control his public or working life, he may have the lion's share of control of the private space he occupies, as a result of his authority as legal husband, legal father, and provider of the material necessities of life. In the only sphere a woman is allowed to be in, she is subject to the control of another.

Males in the lower segment are liable to perform productive work, doing such things as physically planting the seeds, running the machines that make the parts for tractors, computers, and so on. Females in the lower segment also frequently perform such work, but females in both segments, B and B_1, are liable to perform reproductive work. That person does this work who physically feeds and dresses the baby, remains 'on duty' watching the children so long as no one replaces her, and so on.

Marriage has been the legal institution which ensured the dependence of women on men, and of reproductive on productive labour, by making women the property of their husbands who thereby had the right to determine the nature and circumstances of women's labour. While this was almost certainly done in order to perpetuate a system of private property under male ownership, it also had the effect of ensuring that necessary reproductive labour was done, that it was done virtually exclusively by women, and that it was done as cheaply as possible – typically indeed, for nothing.

With increasing industrialization, the emergence of forms of private property other than rights over land and its products, and the diminishing importance of private property in the form of land, the class of men whose property interest was directly served by this system was diminished. Under capitalism only a small minority of men, namely ruling-class males, had a specific need for this system, since only they had any property to worry about. Thus, while this system exploited women as a group, since they were compelled to engage in reproductive labour, it was required for the economic interests of only a few men, though this is not to say that all men did not benefit from it in other ways.

But since, under capitalism, this system is needed primarily to serve the property interest of ruling-class males, this has led Marxists of various stripes to conclude that the oppression of women, insofar as it is linked to private property, is therefore entirely a product of class division. Engels, for example, concluded that in the working class there was no objective basis for the oppression of women, and, therefore, that working class women are not in fact oppressed by working-class men! To the extent that laws generally reflect the needs of the dominant class, the details of the legal structure of marriage and the family have been determined by the need for the regulated inheritance of property, rather than for the need to ensure that necessary reproductive labour would be performed. This explains why the legalities of marriage are in general far more important to the middle and ruling classes, than they are to the lower classes. Where the latter are more proletarianized, which is to say more dependant on low-paying wage work, the inheritance of property such as a home or agricultural land becomes less and less a factor in their lives. Under these circumstances, legal marriage begins to be irrelevant to their real concerns.

Far from being proof of their immorality, as it has been so often held to be, its real significance lies in the fact that male wage workers have little material need, as wage workers, for the legal institution of marriage. Yet working-class women are the ones who do the reproductive work, with or without legal marriage, the operating sanction being their lesser access to remunerative productive labour, which promotes dependence on a male, with or without the legitimization conferred by marriage.

Thus, while working-class men do not need the structure of marriage to preserve a property interest, society as a whole nonetheless profits from the fact that the relationships between men and women are the same among the working class as they are among the propertied classes because working-class women are still performing necessary reproductive labour. It therefore seems clear that the primary material function of the family in the working class is more exclusively determined by the relations and demands of reproduction than of production. And this is not simply by default, that is, through lack of property. It is a result of the fact that this class is the source of society's labour power, making that function of overriding importance. Cheap reproductive labour must still be provided to ensure future sources of cheap productive labour.

Feminism has for the most part taken the form of demanding to be let into sphere A, the productive sphere, from sphere B, the reproductive sphere. This is an important goal. But if our analysis of the two forms of labour needed for the existence of society is correct, it is clear that this can be a solution for no more than a few isolated individuals, so long as the unique liability of women *as a group* to perform reproductive labour remains. Economic and social pressure on women to do this work, and to do it as an act of love or duty rather than of social labour, will continue to be relentless unless and until its organization is fundamentally altered to become democratically shared by all adults in society.

Our analysis of the historical position of women and of the significance of assuming that an adequate political theory must guarantee equality of the sexes suggests several important tasks for political philosophy. First and most importantly, a comprehensive and egalitarian theory of social reproduction must be provided, based on the assumptions that reproductive labour is as *socially* necessary as productive labour and that reproductive labour should be performed at least as voluntarily as productive labour. A second task is the development of an adequate theory of the relation between production and reproduction. (Many different theories are, of course, possible.) But these are the two great challenges to which political theory must respond if it is to be of any future significance.

We hope that the essays in this collection show ample reason for concluding that traditional political theory is utterly bankrupt in the light of present perspectives. We conclude that it is now up to us to remedy this by providing new theories which reflect a deeper understanding of our historical position and a profoundly changed perception of sexual and reproductive reality.

THE SEXISM OF SOCIAL AND POLITICAL THEORY

The Function of Equal Education in Plato's *Republic* and *Laws*

LYNDA LANGE

Plato appears to be inconsistent in his treatment of women. He developed in the *Republic* the idea that males and females should be educated equally for the highest functions, while at the same time he believed that women were ultimately not as good as men. A further difficulty with Plato's views on women occurs as a result of his apparent about-face on the question in the *Laws*. Numerous attempts have been made to resolve these difficulties.

One of the most popular approaches has been to attempt to explain away Plato's so-called feminism. Among those who consider the *Republic* to be purely ideal, and thoroughly impractical, the equality of women and the communal life of the guardians are sometimes considered to be a virtual *reductio ad absurdum* of Plato's views. If *this* is what is required, they argue, obviously such a state could never be and thus Plato could not have intended it as a literal model for the state.[1]

Those who take Plato's position on women seriously have done so on the basis of the arguments in defence of the recommendation that they not be excluded from public life, and that those females showing signs of the capacity to be guardians should be given exactly the same mental and physical education as their male counterparts.[2] It is true that the mere fact that Plato suggested that it was possible that some women have the potential to be guardians distinguishes him markedly from his contemporaries, and indeed from most political thinkers of the past. This is true in spite of the inadequacy of his views from the standpoint of feminism today.

This inadequacy is by no means minor, however. It is apparent, for example, that Plato did not intend that the guardian class be equally divided by sex. According to Plato, women as a class are inferior to men as a class.[3] Therefore, even though some women are superior to some men, proportionately fewer women than men may be expected to attain to the highest level of development that qualifies individuals to be guardians. Indeed, I shall argue below that his recommendations for women do not necessarily imply that *any* of them will become guardians.

There are numerous passages that indicate that Plato did not consider women to be as good as men. For example, in the discussion in Book III of the *Republic* of the best education for those likely to become guardians, Socrates says that if they go in for drama they must imitate only 'men ... who are brave, sober, pious, free,' and not be allowed to imitate women or slaves. It appears from this and other passages, that Plato thought that women, in addition to being weaker in everything, were more likely than men to be cowardly, hysterical, and given to luxury.[4]

In spite of this, however, Plato did not believe that women and men had different social and political functions to fulfil as a result of their having different natures. The difference of sex, according to Plato, is a fact about individuals that is not relevant to their political status, as baldness is not relevant to a man's ability to cobble shoes. There is, nevertheless, a de facto correlation between femaleness and inferiority, as we have seen. What Plato appears to have done with women is allow for exceptions, in much the same way as he allows for exceptions to appear in the otherwise inferior artisan class. Assuming that feminism entails at least the belief that women are 'as good as' men, though not necessarily 'the same as' men, this correlation of femaleness and inferiority is in itself a good reason for saying that Plato is not a feminist, though not my main reason for saying so.[5]

It may be objected that the provision of equal opportunity for education of the sexes is sufficient to earn Plato the ascription of feminist, on the ground that what is wrong with the male supremacist view is not the fact that women are not found in the same numbers as men in every segment of society, from combat training to the judge's bench, but the fact that their exclusion has been arbitrary and unfair. Given rational and fair criteria for the assignment of social functions, the argument runs, women and men will assume functions appropriate to their individual abilities, which may or may not result in equal numbers in a given field of activity. While the application of rational criteria is of major importance in the structure of the *Republic*, Plato's concept of justice involves no idea of fairness. The amount of attention now paid to the arguments in *Republic* v that it is possible for women to be educated in the same way as men may be partly accounted for by the unexamined modern assumption that if it is *possible* for people to function as equals, then it is self-evidently desirable for them to do so. I do not think Plato would have shared this assumption. He thought democracy was possible, for example, but quite undesirable. There is no indication that concern for fairness or equality was his motive for suggesting that women not be excluded from any social function. In other words, it was not equal participation *for women* in the good life he was concerned about, but some other good for the whole city. This interpretation is consistent with his stated position that the good of the city as a whole is his basic criterion for making judgments, and not the good of the guardian class.[6]

I shall argue that his position on women cannot be properly understood as feminist, no matter how inconsistently so it may be. I believe his position to be philosophically interesting, however, because it seems to be addressed to a profound problem of political theory still very much at issue. This is the contradiction between public and private life which exists where there is a social structure and an ideology that separates the two.

I shall argue at the same time that the inadequacy of his position from the standpoint of current feminism is not fatal to his views (from a logical point of view), because his purposes in making the recommendations concerning women do not require unqualified identity of worth between the sexes or strict quantitative equality such as equal numbers in the guardian class. His theoretical concerns are ultimately not those of feminism.

Before proceeding to further examination of Plato, I shall explain my use of the terms 'public' and 'private,' and what is meant by saying that there is a contradiction between them.

The distinction between the public sphere of activity and the private sphere has been present in all political theory which has attempted to be comprehensive, although the terminology for it varies. Whatever is considered distinctively political activity, such as economic or productive activity of a certain type (for example, that paid for by a wage) – is 'public.' This is contrasted with whatever is deemed non-political, personal, natural, biological, and so on, all of which may be catagorized as 'private.' The delineation of this distinction is a subject for inquiry in itself, and no more than a brief discussion will be presented here.

The concepts 'public' and 'private' are linked together; they cannot be understood except in relation to each other. Nothing can be understood to be 'public,' unless something is 'private,' and *vice versa*. Each concept contains implicit normative prescriptions for behaviour in its realm and the realm of the other, and also implies the reservation of something to itself. There is also assumed to be a difference in value and importance between the two spheres.

In societies where this dichotomy is maintained, there is a constant opposition between the requirements of public life (for example, for a person in pursuit of a career) and private life (for example, for a parent). This opposition occurs on both the practical and conceptual level. The private or family sphere is associated conceptually with what are usually conceived of as the 'natural,' or even 'instinctive,' impulses of human beings for companionship, sex, children, emotional expression, and so on. This is in contrast to the structure of civil society, which is usually considered a product of human artifice, and a matter of convention. The 'natural' impulses have often been deemed non-rational, if not positively irrational, whereas the ability to fulfill the duties of a citizen has been tied, at least in theory, to the ability either to transcend or to control one's non-rational impulses by means of reason or intelligence.

Most importantly, role differentiation between the sexes has histori- cally always been articulated as a difference in the duties owed to the state or to economic productivity, and those owed to a particular family. The former duties are basic for men, and the latter are basic for women. The supposed superiority of public, and productive activity is the ideo- logical source of the authority of the male within the private family. His authority ensures that the functions of the family are fulfilled in such a way that their tendency to run counter to the functions of the state is well contained. The male head of a family is virtually a representative within the family of the value system of public life. This helps to explain why those who recommend the elimination of private families, such as Plato, usually also recommend a fairly high degree of state authority over sexual relations and reproduction. The heads of families must con- stantly adjudicate between the rival demands of the two spheres, which to me hints at the explanation of Plato's alleged feminism.

I believe Plato's true philosophical concern in recommending equal education is ultimately derived from his concept of justice, although it is helpful to consider some crucial historical features of Greek society as well. This approach removes both of the apparent inconsistencies in his views on women.

Plato's concept of social justice is briefly defined by Socrates as the per- formance by each individual of the work for which he is best suited.[7]

Equally important, however, if the structure of the city is to be recognizably Plato's, is his hierarchical arrangement of functions. While it is just for each individual to perform the functions, no matter how menial, for which he is best suited, this by no means entails for Plato an equality of value among functions. The functions which are considered by Plato to be noble and worth pursuing for their own sake are only a small portion of the functions that are needed for the existence of a just city. In fact, *all* of the functions needed for the physical maintenance of the city are inferior functions to be done by the inferior artisan class. The physical defence of the city is consigned to a group of medium value.

In the *Republic* the functions of the guardian class are very closely analogous to the functions of the human mind within the framework of strict dualism. The distinctively human virtue of justice can really only be attributed to those whose 'work' is a work of the mind, namely philosophic wisdom. This is because justice is initially defined as a property of the whole city insofar as it is ruled by the wisdom of the guardian class, which thereby performs its proper function and ensures that the other parts perform theirs. The analogy between the justice of the city and the justice of the individual only holds for the members of the guardian class. They are the only individuals self-ruled by intelligence in the same manner in which the city is ruled. The members of other classes, while they are exhorted to moderation, are nevertheless dominated by either appetite or spirit, neither of which are said to be uniquely human traits.

The starting position for Socrates' defence of this concept of justice in the *Republic* is the conviction that the division of labour is better than the performance by each individual of the work necessary for his or her own maintenance. One basic criterion appears to be simple efficiency. Socrates says 'more things are produced and better and more easily when one man performs one task according to his nature, at the right moment, and at leisure from other occupations.'[8] One could grant to Plato that people's natures suit them to different tasks without being compelled to conclude that they ought not to be allowed to work at any other task. For that conclusion, either a criterion of efficiency or some other additional criterion is needed. The application to production of a standard based on the Platonic virtue of performing well the task for which one is best suited would be almost indistinguishable in practice from the criterion of efficiency. It would be interesting to speculate as to whether there were features of the Greek mode of production emerging in Plato's day that prompted him to think in these terms. For the purposes of this paper, however, we need only note that a hierarchical division of labour was an elementary feature of his political philosophy, before we go on to see how he uses that idea.

He projects this idea onto the individual soul, where it takes the form of a hierarchy of functions for the parts of the soul. From this it follows easily enough that the best functioning of these parts requires attention to one of them to the exclusion of the others. Practical concerns, as functions of the appetitive soul, were considered ignoble. As such their performance was a positive obstacle to the highest development of intelligence. Courage as well, though better than appetite, was still subordinate to intelligence. According to Plato, it was desirable to have as complete a division of these functions as possible. This general train of thought also helps to account for Plato's view of ruling as a specialized 'craft,'[9] by analogy with the division of labour in production. This view is by no means self-evident.

The division of functions between social classes, such as that among the artisan, soldier, and guardian classes, is a necessary measure for enabling some to be free of the toil of practical concerns. But this division only accounts for the productive requirements of society and not the reproductive requirements. If it is noted that human reproduction requires nurture and socialization of dependent individuals for a long period of time, and not just birth, then it follows that this activity comprises a large percentage of the labour expended by adults in society. Hence, if it is good for 'the best' to be free from practical concerns, they must be free from the responsibility and trouble of caring for children.[10]

In the history of political theory, the almost universal response to this question of reproduction is to designate the female companions of such men (and females in general) as the ones who ought rightly to perform this task. But Plato avoids this approach completely. It is perhaps not surprising that the explanation for this anomaly may be found in his equally anomalous concept of justice.

His reasons for believing that the guardians should have absolutely no private property turn out to be the same as his reasons for recommending that women and children be 'in common.' In Book III of the *Republic* Socrates argues that in addition to a proper education, the guardians should have houses and possessions provided for them in such a way as to avoid the evils of interfering with the best performance of their work as guardians, or inciting them to wrong other citizens. To avoid this, none must have any private property and literally no private place. The ownership of houses and lands, according to Plato, automatically means 'hating and being hated, plotting being plotted against'; he goes even farther in declaring that private ownership is positively incompatible with guardianship, and transforms guardians from helpers to 'enemies and masters.'[11]

The self-governance of the guardians, and their totally disinterested rule of the city, require total dedication to the understanding of eternal truths. All personal and private concerns are obstacles to the attainment of these goals. It is virtually a corollary of this that attachment to other individuals, whether sexual lovers, husbands, wives, parents, or children, is also an impediment to this type of personal development. In addition, the total absence of private places and belongings in itself almost precludes the existence of a 'private family.' I think Plato was aware of these consequences and this may be why he has Socrates casually mention in the same book (Book IV) that for the guardians women and children will be in common.[12]

When this question is examined in detail in Book V, the challenge to Socrates appears to be the question of whether or not it is possible for selected men and women to have the same education and functions. These are the arguments that have received most of the scholarly attention from persons interested in Plato's apparent 'feminism.' Yet proof that the performance of these functions by women is possible is merely the first step. There must also be arguments to show that it is feasible for women and children to be in common to the male guardians,[13] and most important, arguments to show that these things are beneficial to the city. Socrates postpones the question of feasibility, never to return to it, and proceeds to argue that the absence of private families is beneficial.

Plato consistently uses the language of property relations in discussing this question.[14] This is further evidence for the view that his philosophical concerns cannot properly be called feminist. If Plato were a feminist but merely inconsistent, it strikes me as unlikely that the inconsistency would be quite that gross, especially since the ethical question of ownership of one person by another was a familiar one to Plato. Women and children, according to Plato, must not be *privately owned* by the guardians, but must be held in common. That he considered the ownership of property and of private wives and children almost identical in nature is apparent from passages such as the following: 'these present prescriptions prevent them from distracting the city by referring *mine* not to the same but to different things, one man dragging off to his own house anything he is able to acquire apart from the rest ... and having women and children apart, thus introducing into the state the pleasures and pains of individuals.'[15] His reservations about the actual worth of women are suggested by the passage in which Socrates says the lawgiver will 'select to give over to (these men) women *as nearly as possible* of the same nature' (my emphasis).[16] If the equality of the sexes were Plato's theoretical concern, he would not have written such a passage.

The greatest good for the city, according to Plato, is that which promotes unity, and the greatest cause of disunity is 'when the citizens do not utter in unison such words as "mine" and "not mine."' Private marriage is a powerful opponent of unity in this sense, being an endless source of particular, individual interests not shared by the citizens as a group. Plato states very clearly the opposition of private and public life when he writes that ideally the citizens should 'rejoice and grieve alike at the same births and deaths,' and that 'the individualization of these feelings is a dissolvent.'[18] Plato's opinion that wives and children should be 'in common' is therefore partly explained by the very oppression of women in Greek society. To the extent that they were virtually pieces of property, it seemed to Plato that they should be held in common like other property.

Interestingly, only at this point does Socrates offer an answer to the long-postponed question of what makes the guardians happy. Once again he groups together property and family relations: 'I hesitate, so unseemly are they, even to mention the pettiest troubles of which they would be rid, the flatterings of the rich, the embarrassments and pains of the poor in the bringing-up of their children and the procuring of money for the necessities of life for their households, ... and all the indignities that they endure in such matters, which are obvious and ignoble and not deserving of mention.'[19] Being free of all these concerns, and having the honour of the city, the guardians are said to lead the happiest of lives.

There is some evidence that Plato regarded particular family attachments among the rulers as even more of a threat to the unity of the city than private property, for he names the community of women and children as *the cause* of the unity of the state.[20] Socrates draws an analogy between the unified state and a single living organism, but it appears that the more accurate analogy is between the state and the biological family. It is logically impossible for the guardians to 'have one experience of pleasure and pain,' but they can have the feelings of loyalty and identity of interest identified with the family, albeit in a moderated form. In arguing for the benefits of his scheme, Socrates suggests that no guardian could think of another as an outsider, because 'no matter whom he meets, he will feel that he is meeting a brother, a sister, a father, a mother, a son, a daughter.' Plato has attempted to remove the contradiction between public and private life for the guardians by raising familial impulses from the private to the public sphere, where their effect is to promote unity in the state, rather than disunity. These sentiments are thereby transformed in theory from the particular interests of individuals to the level of generality appropriate for citizens.

Since there are to be no monogamous relationships in the guardian class, and all sexual intercourse is to be strictly controlled for eugenic reasons, there is no need for equal numbers of men and women. The best age (20-40) for females to have children is over before the age of guardianship; for men the best age to reproduce is 30 to 55. Obviously Plato was assuming that male guardians would be mated with promising young females, who might or might not subsequently become guardians. The problem for the state of the private family has been eliminated without necessarily granting equality of worth or the full participation in government to both sexes.

The separation of sex and love which is briefly discussed in *Republic* III 21 also supports this interpretation. It is strikingly appropriate for this scheme that when sex and love are separated they both become non-exclusive. Non-sexual love may plausibly extend to all the members of a small community, especially in the rational form that Plato regarded as 'the right' love: 'sober and harmonious love of the orderly and the beautiful.' And sex, denigrated as a mere pleasure of appetite, also becomes non-exclusive. It is the combination of sex and love that is likely to create the 'madness' and 'extravagant pleasure,' as well as the personal attachments, so inimical to virtue and the good of the state. Their separation, besides rendering them non-exclusive, also makes them more appropriately moderate.

In the *Laws*, Plato's recommendations for marriage, sex, and child-rearing are considerably different. Plato has moved from his extraordinary ideas of communal sexual relations and child care to an insistence on strict monogamous marriage. In spite of this apparent about-face, a common strand of thought may be picked up in the reasons he offers in the *Laws* for these different institutions.

There is a passage in the *Laws* which suggests that Plato had *not* changed his mind on these questions since writing the *Republic*, but for some reason felt impelled to offer a less radical scheme of regulations. In the course of discussing the education of both sexes he writes: 'Now if we are going to look for an exact realization of our scheme, as we have styled it, it will perhaps never be found, so long as there are private wives, children, and houses ... Still, if we can secure the second-best conditions, which we are now describing, we shall indeed come off well enough.'[22] As in the *Republic*, Plato has grouped together the having of property and the having of wives and children, and has thus not progressed beyond his earlier intuition that wives and children 'belong to' men. The function of the 'second-best' conditions of marriage and procreation is to ameliorate as far as possible the destructive effects of private families on the city.

According to the Athenian: 'While the right regulation of the private households within a society is neglected, it is idle to expect the foundation of public law to be secure.'[23] It appears there are several evils liable to befall a city where a private family life is considered a thing apart from public life. For these evils two sources are named. One is simple privacy in the descriptive sense. 'The privacy of home life,' he writes, 'screens from the general observation many little incidents ... which are not in keeping with a legislator's recommendations.'[24] A private upbringing may produce a character which is not appropriate for citizens. This is important because of the primacy of education in Plato's political philosophy.

The other source of evil is the character of women as a group. According to the Athenian, women are 'inclined to secrecy and craft' and ought not to be 'left to their disorders.'[25] Whereas Hegel regarded women as a permanent 'enemy within the gates,'[26] Plato appears to have felt that the enemy could be co-opted by making education and the rewards of public life open to them. The *Laws* contains several passages condemning the luxury and worthlessness of women left to their own devices. There is also the observation that 'her native disposition is inferior to man's,'[27] which is offered as a reason why women ought to be *in*cluded in the public table. Plato once again gives no consideration to the most common opinion about this, which has been the imposition of male authority on the family. The fact that this is not even discussed is even more surprising in the *Laws* than it is in the *Republic*, because so many of the conventional trappings of marriage are left untouched in the *Laws*. For example, there is the 'right of valid betrothal' by the father, and the payment of dowries, and so on.[28] But even these activities are somewhat altered in nature by the ubiquitous laws, all of which are intended to direct everything for the general good of the city.

There is a suggestion that Plato still considered it desirable for 'the best' to transcend as far as possible the limitations of the 'natural' social companionship of the biological family. The Athenian is asked to justify his position that women ought to participate in the public table. To do so, he reverts to the most basic principles, observing that there are three universal needs: food, drink, and sex. These, he says, are 'unwholesome' in their uneducated condition, and must be diverted from the pleasurable to the good.[29]

This citing of basic principles, however, is not followed up by the sort of profound argument for the inclusion of women in public life that we had been led to expect. What follows is a prescription for the tight regulation and minute supervision of marriage and procreation, in order to divert sexual desire from the pleasurable to the good. Plato does not make explicit the connection between this and the inclusion of women in public life. Detailed regulation of sexual relations does not in itself entail that women and men should perform the same social functions. However, a massive attempt is being made to redirect the activities which have the greatest tendency to be intensely personal and individual concerns. For example, a man must 'court the (marital) tie that is for the city's good, not that which most takes his own fancy.'[30] Plato obviously felt that the redirection of these sentiments would not be possible so long as women were excluded from public life, though the connection is obscure in the Laws.

The following argument, which is consistent with the interpretation made of the Republic as well, may make this connection coherent. So long as men and women are unequal in society, and women are confined to private, family life, any regulation of the family will inevitably be imposed through the authority of the husband. To the extent that there is public supervision of the family, the authority of the husband and father is undermined. By the same token, so long as he is the enforcer, he retains the authority, with its accompanying benefits to him within the private sphere, and his family concerns are an individual pursuit. Such authority requires some material base, which means economic responsibility on his part for the needs of the family. This further reinforces the separation of public and private duties between the sexes. This introduces all the contradictions which Plato has attempted to avoid in connection with reproduction.

Plato has replaced the total elimination of private life for the guardians recommended in the Republic by tight regulation of it in the Laws, but the desired effect seems to me to be the same. Whereas in the Republic he was prepared to insist on the complete absence of contradictory tendencies between public and private life in the city, in the Laws he attempts rather to ameliorate them and control them.

NOTES AND REFERENCES

1 Allan Bloom, for example, takes this position in his Interpretive Essay which prefaces his translation of Plato's *Republic* (New York 1968), following Leo Strauss in *The City and Man* (Chicago 1964). I.M. Crombie, in *An Examination of Plato's Doctrines* I (New York 1962), writes that Plato's discussion of the equality of women 'should be read by connoisseurs of *a priori* absurdity' (100).

2 For example, Christine Garside Allen 'Plato on Women' *Feminist Studies* II 2/3 (1975), and 'Can a Woman be Good in the Same Way as a Man?' *Dialogue* X 3 (1971); Christine Pierce 'Equality: *Republic* V' *Monist* LVII (Jan. 1973).

3 Edith Hamilton and Huntington Cairns eds *Plato: The Collected Dialogues* (Princeton 1973) 455, 781a

4 Ibid 395 c-e, 455 c-e, 469d

5 See Julia Annas 'Plato's *Republic* and Feminism' *Philosophy* LI (1976) 307–21. She observes 'Now it is hardly a feminist argument to claim that women do not have a special sphere because men can outdo them at absolutely everything' (307).

6 *Dialogues: Republic* 466a

7 Ibid 433a

8 Ibid 370c

9 Ibid 421c

10 The analysis here is based on the theory of reproduction outlined in Lynda Lange 'Reproduction in Democratic Theory' in J. King-Farlow and W. Shea eds *Contemporary Issues in Political Philosophy* (New York 1976).

11 *Republic* 416d, 417b

12 Ibid 424a

13 Ibid 457d

14 Ibid 424a, 453d, 457d, 458c

15 Ibid 464c-d

16 Ibid 458c

17 Ibid 462c

18 Ibid 462b

19 Ibid 465c

20 Ibid 463c, 464b and d

21 Ibid 403a-c

22 *Dialogues: Laws* 807b

23 Ibid 790b

24 Ibid 788a

25 Ibid 781a
26 Hegel *The Phenomenonology of Mind* tr J.B. Baillie (New York 1967) 468
27 *Laws* 781a
28 Ibid 774d-e
29 Ibid 782d-783a
30 Ibid 773b

Women and Locke:
Who owns the apples in the
Garden of Eden?

LORENNE M.G. CLARK

The idea of creating a society guaranteeing equality between the sexes has never been considered by most political theorists. They have either endorsed, or simply accepted, the assumption of a natural inequality of the sexes which ought to be preserved in civil society.[1] This same presupposition has excluded the family from the theorists' framework of what are thought to be distinctively *political* institutions. Despite the central role of the family in human life, it has been consigned to the domain of purely natural phenomena. The related belief that women and children must be relegated for theoretical purposes to the family, to be safely ignored in a realm of brute nature, suffices to allow such theorists to exclude women from the ontology of politics (except insofar as they do productive work).

In looking at major theorists from this perspective, the task is not simply to show that they display sexist attitudes. The main purpose is to demonstrate that their theories rest on these assumptions and that they would be vastly different theories if these assumptions were not made. The point of such a demonstration is to establish that the theories which have been advanced on these foundations are not workable as blueprints for political institutions guaranteeing sexual equality. It remains to show how major political theorists demonstrate these assumptions, what use they make, either explicitly or implicitly, of these premisses, and what problems this causes in their theories.

I wish to examine Locke from this point of view. To what extent does Locke illustrate the basic sexist assumptions which I have argued lie at the foundation of western political theory? The specific premisses I take to be central to western political theory are, first, that there is a 'natural' inequality of the sexes and a 'natural' superiority of the male; second, that reproduction is not a central fact of political life and is of no value in creating a significant life for man; and, third, that the family is not a political, but a 'natural' institution which remains outside the political framework in an ahistorical state of nature.

In addition to these major assumptions, there are further minor or derivative hypotheses which require examination. Among these, and of particular relevance to Locke, are questions relating to inheritance and the ownership of property. How do Locke's major premises function to justify ownership and inheritance of private property in order to preserve dominant sex and class position? Is ownership of the means and products of reproduction, as well as those of production, really needed to generate the kind of political society which Locke thinks is needed to secure 'the peace, safety, and public good of the people' which is, he argues, the end of government?[2]

The first assumption, that there is an inequality of the sexes and that the male is superior, is both implicit and explicit in Locke. In the *First Treatise*, in attempting to refute Filmer's claim that Adam rules over Eve by dint of the law of God, Locke is at great pains to show that the source of the condition in which women are subjugated to men does not lie in law, but in nature: 'Farther it is to be noted, that these words here of 3 *Gen.* 16 which our A. calls the Original Grant of Government were not spoken to Adam, neither indeed was there any Grant in them made to Adam, but a Punishment laid upon Eve; and if we will take them as they were directed in particular to her, or in her, as their representative to all other Women, they will at most concern the Female Sex only, and import no more but that Subjection they should ordinarily be in to their Husbands: But there is here no more Law to oblige a Woman to such a Subjection, if the Circumstances either of her Condition or Contract with her Husband should exempt her from it, then there is, that she should bring forth her Children in Sorrow and Pain, if there could be found a Remedy for it, which is also a part of the same Curse upon her.'[3]

Thus the subjection in which most women are ordinarily found with respect to men is explicitly not the result of law, or any sort of arbitrary convention, not even that most Divine convention established by the will and authority of God. Rather it lies in the punishment laid on her, and on her alone, which consists in her being, as he says later in the same passage, 'the weaker Sex,' and forced to bring forth children in pain and sorrow.

Women are, then, by nature weaker than men, and this weakness is itself a direct result of the unique capacities women have with respect to reproduction. The Curse of God laid on women consists in her being by nature disadvantaged, and the disadvantage is clearly considered to be her reproductive capacities. The fact that women and women alone can bear children is a natural disadvantage which leads to a natural inequality between the sexes. Despite the fact that Locke believes that the inequality of the sexes is contingent, grounded in natural differences between the sexes with respect to reproduction, this nonetheless establishes the superiority of the male: For though as a helper in the Temptation, as well as a Partner in the Transgression, Eve was laid below him, and so he had accidentally a Superiority over her.[4]

But given that there is this natural inequality, the common condition of women is to be under the subjection of men. However, precisely because this is a natural inequality, it is one which can, on rare occasions, be overcome. Should she be of noble birth, or ample means, these qualities compensate for her natural disadvantages, and she can, by means of these qualities, escape the condition of subjugation to which she would otherwise be liable: 'And will any one say, that Eve, or any other Woman sinn'd, if she were brought to Bed without those multiplied Pains God threatens her here with? Or that either of our Queens Mary or Elizabeth, had they Married any of their Subjects, had been by this Text put into a Political Subjection to him? or that he thereby should have had Monarchical Rule over her? God, in this Text gives not, that I see, any Authority to Adam over Eve, or to Men over their Wives, but only foretells what should be Womans Lot, how by his Providence he would order it so, that she should be subject to her husband, as we see that generally the Laws of Mankind and customs of Nations have ordered it so; and there is, I grant, a Foundation in Nature for it.'[5] Locke explicitly here acknowledges that the subjection of women to men is codified in law and custom. But he finds its source in nature and is, by this means, able to argue that in some few instances it is a natural liability which can be overcome.

Locke's objective in chapter v of the *First Treatise*, 'Of Adam's Title to Sovereignty by the Subjection of Eve,' is to show that God's creation of a natural basis for inequality between the sexes does not establish any basis, natural or otherwise, for Absolute Sovereignty and the absolute duty of obedience Filmer alleges to exist between subjects and monarch. The most Genesis establishes, says Locke, are 'the Subjection of the Inferior Ranks of Creatures to Mankind,' (1:28) and 'the Subjection that is due from a Wife to her Husband' (3:16).[6] Thus he neither questions nor criticizes the alleged basis of the inequality and endorses the assumption that the natural difference between the sexes leads to the creation of an obligation on the part of a wife to be subjected to the will and authority of her husband: it is what is *due* from her to him.

In the *Second Treatise*, in 'Of Paternal Power,' he states that 'though I have said above that all men by nature are equal, I cannot be supposed to understand all sorts of equality.' He cites age, virtue, excellence of parts and merit, birth, alliance, and benefits as differences in respect of which some men gain a precedence over others. He goes on to say that none of these differences in respect of which men are not in some sense equal, conflicts with the way in which they are equal, namely, 'in respect of jurisdiction or dominion one over another ... that equal right that every man has to his natural freedom, without being subjected to the will or authority of any other men.'[7]

Thus Locke does not deny that there are differences among men.[8] He argues instead that men are equal with respect to the right to autonomy *despite* these differences. However, as we have already seen, the allegedly 'natural' differences between the sexes do justify the natural domination of women by men. His explicit statement on this issue in the *Second Treatise* is as follows: 'it therefore being necessary that the last determination – i.e., the rule – should be somewhere, it naturally falls to the man's share, as the abler and the stronger.'[9] The rule *naturally* falls to the man's share. Here he stresses that it is man's natural superiority (by virtue of his being 'abler and the stronger'), rather than woman's natural disadvantage, which gives rise to men's rightful rule over women. I agree here with Elrington, who says that this implies that the right of the husband arises solely from superior power. There are more similarities between Locke and Hobbes than are sometimes assumed.[10]

Two things are immediately obvious from this. In the *First Treatise* Locke appeared to argue that it is simply as a consequence of women's natural disadvantage that men do, as a matter of fact, ordinarily rule over women, but in the end he concludes that wives have a duty to obey. Thus there is a curious asymmetry between the sexes with respect to the consequences which follow from the fact that there are differences, natural and otherwise, between one person and another. The presupposition of a fundamental right to autonomy overrides any differences which may exist between individual men.

The natural differences between the sexes, however, override any presupposition of an equal right to autonomy for men and women. Here and only here a natural difference creates a justified domination of one person by another. However, the existence of clearly non-natural differences between one woman and another may sometimes override the presumption of female inferiority which explains and justifies the general subjugation of women by men. Thus, exceptional women may, because of the presence of social differences, overcome their natural disadvantage and so escape subjection. But in general the natural differences between men and women overrule any presupposition of equality between the sexes. Differences between individual men do not negate the presumption of equality among men, and differences between individual women may overcome the presumption of inferiority and so create a right to autonomy in some cases.

It seems abundantly clear, however, that Locke believed that there was a natural inequality between the sexes, that men were superior, and that this superiority ordinarily gave them a right to the obedience of their wives. It also seems clear that he believed that the source of women's inferiority lay in their reproductive capacities, and that he regarded this as a natural rather than a conventional disadvantage. It must be pointed out, however, that it is difficult to say that Locke saw this as the sole source and nature of women's inferior status. It is far from clear what her reproductive disadvantage has to do with the 'greater strength' and being 'abler' he attributes to males and which he uses to justify the authority of husband over wife in the *Second Treatise*.

How these assumptions affected the development of his theory can best be seen by considering how they shaped his assumptions about the family and its relation to other, political, institutions. Throughout both treatises Locke assumes that the natural condition of women is to be in the family. The subjection of women by men is the subjection of wife by husband. He nowhere discusses the status of the single woman. Women are, for Locke, married women, and, hence, most women are under the subjection of men. And most women are married women, because it is woman's nature to reproduce children which she is incapable of providing for on her own.[11] When he discusses the role of women, he explicitly states that they were created as companions for men and that they are incapable of bearing and rearing children without the assistance of men at least until all of the children are, as he says, 'out of a dependency for support.' Thus it is the natural fate of women to be married as a consequence of their reproductive capacities, and to be under the subjection of their husbands because they are dependent on them for the support of their offspring. Locke thus assumes that the family and its structure of authority are a natural association created in the state of nature.

The problem for Locke was then to distinguish political authority from natural authority. Political authority must rest on consent and, hence, must be distinguished and distinguishable from natural familial authority which rests on a natural superiority of the male over the female which is itself grounded in a natural difference between them with respect to their reproductive roles.

In discussing the beginning of political societies, Locke admits that most civil societies began under the government and administration of one man: 'the government commonly began in the father, for the father, having by the law of nature the same power with every man else to punish as he thought fit any offenses against that law, might thereby punish his transgressing children even when they were men.'[12] This is an *admission* for Locke because, for other reasons which we know very well, he was out to attack the concept of patriarchal government but nonetheless had to acknowledge the historical fact that most governments began as forms of paternal power and were, therefore, patriarchal governments. He did not want legitimate government to hang on the natural dominion man has in the family.

The interesting and important point to be seen is that since he himself assumes that male dominion in the family is natural, he must show that paternal power is to be distinguished from political power in order to argue that the basis for legitimate government is consent. Since he assumed that in the state of nature men exercised a natural dominion over women, he could hardly argue that even patriarchal dominion in the family is artificial and so cannot be used to justify patriarchal concepts of government. This would have been the most believable argument to advance to effect that conclusion. But he did not use it, and that is just the point. So far as he was concerned, that position was of no use. He simply assumes that the family and the division of power within it are a natural and not a political creation. As will become apparent, what is even more important is that he *must* assume this in order to arrive at a theory of society which conforms to the principles he thinks it must.

In the state of nature, women are naturally disadvantaged, men are naturally superior, and the family arises as a natural institution based on these natural differences between the sexes.[13] Thus, everything he says about equality in the state of nature pertains only to men. Men, and men only, are naturally free from the dominion of one over another, though this is consistent with his belief that some women do manage to maintain some measure of control over their lives and their property.[14] The vast majority of women are already under the domination of individual men because they are 'naturally' weaker and less able. They share the common natural disadvantage to which all women are subject, and have none of the compensating virtues to offset their natural liability and so place them in a position where they do not have to accept the will and authority of men in order to survive. Thus, Locke's hypothetical state of nature is as full of presumptions about the different reproductive natures and relations of the sexes as it is about the different productive natures and relations of men, which have been so often and so thoroughly dealt with by others.[15] Locke's state of nature is simply seventeenth-century England devoid of legitimate Lockean law and authority.

However, in his attempts to undermine the concept of patriarchal government Locke was forced to take a somewhat less conservative view of the relations between the sexes in the family than might otherwise have been the case. He also cites anthropological evidence which in fact challenges his unrecognized assumptions about sexual inequality in the state of nature. But of course he did not draw from these any conclusions as to the conventional nature of existing familial relationships.

His basic argument in chapter IV, 'Of Paternal Power,' in the *Second Treatise*, is that no support for patriarchal government can be derived from the existence of paternal power in the family because the power in the family, which consists in the exercise of parental authority over children, is equally shared between father and mother. He argues that 'paternal' power is really a misnomer, and should be replaced with 'parental' power, because 'paternal' 'seems so to place the power of parents over their children wholly in the father, as if the mother had no share in it; whereas, if we consult reason or revelation, we shall find she has an equal title.'[16] He hardly mentions the dominion of husband over wife. He did not see this as relevant to his attack on patriarchal government. He wanted to establish that no one man, by right and without consent, could rule over another, not that no one man by right could rule over a woman. He assumed that men would continue to exercise dominion over women in the political as well as the familial sphere, and so there was no need to question the authority of husband over wife.

But it was important to him to show that the father did not have absolute authority over his children. As he puts the case himself: 'it will but very ill serve the turn of those men who contend so much for the absolute power and authority of the fatherhood, as they call it, that the mother should have any share in it; and it would have but ill supported the monarchy they contend for, when by the very name it appeared that

that fundamental authority from whence they would derive their government of a single person only was not placed in one but two persons jointly.' Thus, the family provides no justification for one-man rule in government because the authority over children devolves on two persons.

The joint authority of parents is, however, a theme he relentlessly repeats, and in fact, he goes as far as he can in denigrating the authority over children which paternity legitimizes, in order to undermine as far as possible patriarchal concepts of what constitutes legitimate government: 'But what reason can hence advance this care of the parents due to their offspring into an absolute arbitrary dominion of the father, whose power reaches no farther than ... to give such strength and health to their bodies ... as may best fit his children to be most useful to themselves and others ... But in this power the mother, too, has her share with the father. Nay, this power so little belongs to the father by any peculiar right of nature, but only as he is guardian of his children, that when he quits his care of them he loses his power over them ... so little power does the bare act of begetting give a man over his issue.' Mere fatherhood establishes nothing, says Locke. Authority, in this case, proceeds not from simple paternity but from the acceptance of responsibility – and so, of course he wants to say, in government. Notice, too, that he here wishes to construe the parental role as one of *guardianship*, which is certainly more applicable to civil than to natural relationships. In his enthusiasm to denaturalize politics, he verges on politicizing the family.

One could, in fact, push this somewhat further. While he has said elsewhere that the power of a husband over his wife is one form of power a man can have,[17] he wants to distinguish it both from the power a father has over his children, and the power a magistrate has over his subjects. Only the latter is *political* power. But more importantly for our point here, only a father's power over his children presents us with a relationship in any way relevant to a consideration of the nature and limits of political power. The relationship between husband and wife, in which the husband is in the superior position, does not even have to be justified as does the power of a father over his children. That form of power simply comes about as a result of a natural inequality which, unlike that between parents and children, does not disappear through time and tutelage. This is a natural dominion of one sex over the other.

Thus the relationship between parents and children is more like the relationship between a legitimate sovereign and his subjects. It is a limited power in which the period of dominion is grounded on natural inequalities which disappear over time. Of course, it is unlike legitimate sovereignty in that the latter never licenses an absolute authority since there are no natural inequalities of even a temporary sort between the persons so organized: 'But these two powers, political and paternal, are so perfectly distinct and separate, are built upon so different foundations, and given to so much different ends, that every subject that is a father has as much a paternal power over his children as the prince has over his, and every prince that has parents owes them as much filial duty and obedience as the meanest of his subjects do theirs, and cannot therefore contain any part or degree of that kind of dominion which a prince or magistrate has over his subjects.'

Thus, while Locke rejects 'paternal' in favour of 'parental,' he is deliberately distinguishing 'paternal' power from the power of husband over wife. While we may now have a better name for the relationship existing between father and children, we now have no name to refer to the relationship between husband and wife! It almost ceases to be a power relationship, since it is not seen as a species of power deserving a unique name. In any case, both a father's power over his children and political power are to be contrasted with the power of husband over wife, which, clearly, does not change over time. This is not, of course, an argument which Locke makes, but it obviously lies behind his thinking. If it did not, he would not have advanced his attack on patriarchal government by an analysis of the parental role of a father vis-à-vis his children. Further, he would not have construed patriarchal power as exclusively parental power; he would have invoked as well the relation of husband and wife.

In his zeal to find arguments against patriarchal government his rudimentary anthropology almost gets him too far, however: 'And what will become of this paternal power in that part of the world where one woman has more than one husband at a time, or in those parts of America where, when the husband and wife part, which happens frequently, the children are all left to the mother, follow her, and are wholly under her care and provision?' He does not go the whole way here and begin to question the assumed naturalness of monogamy and male dominance, but the implications are clear that he believes that there are some real 'states of nature' in which even the dominion of male over female does not exist.

However, it must be said that he does at times seem to be aware that the dominion of husband over wife poses something of a problem for his arguments against patriarchal government. He does, for example, argue that marriage is a contractual relationship: 'Conjugal society is made by a voluntary compact between man and woman.' Thus, he is trying to make marriage as analogous as possible to his view of legitimate government. Just as legitimate authority rests on the consent of the governed, so the authority of husband over wife is legitimized by her consent. And he allows that the power of a husband over a wife is not unlimited: 'the power of the husband being so far from that of an absolute monarch that the wife has in many cases a liberty to separate from him where natural right or their contract allows it, whether that contract be made by themselves in the state of nature, or by the customs or laws of the country they live in; and the children upon such separation fall to the father's or mother's lot, as such contract does determine.' He also stresses that it is the obligation of both parents to care for their offspring: 'God having made the parents instruments in his great design of continuing the race of mankind and the occasion of life to their children, as he has laid on them an obligation to nourish, preserve, and bring up their offspring.' He explains monogamy on the basis of the fact that infant human beings require more nurture than the offspring of other animals: 'the father, who is bound to take care for those he has begot, is under an obligation to continue in conjugal society with the same woman longer than other creatures whose young being able to subsist of themselves before the time of procreation returns again, the conjugal bond dissolves of itself and they are at liberty.'

Thus, it is apparently a natural duty that a father should provide for those he has helped to create, and, hence, it could reasonably be maintained that it is a natural right of women to be assisted in the raising of the young they bear. But since he also believes that women, like the females of other animals who give birth to their young alive, are incapable of providing on their own for their offspring, it is clear that they do not have much option but to get married if they desire to have children or if they find they are going to have a child (whether they desire the child or not).

It certainly did not occur to him that a woman could avoid the problem of having yet another child before the others are 'out of a dependency for support' simply by refusing, as a right, to share the marriage bed. His view is simply that it is women's lot to be 'companions' for men who would otherwise be lonely. But clearly it isn't loneliness that he thought would be the problem, however piously he may paper it over with talk about God's grand design for the continuity of the species and the innate ability of man to care for himself. He realized that, as an

unavoidable consequence of men's appetite for more than companionship, women would be with child. He at least had the good grace to insist
on the duty of a biological father to look after his own.

Given his own strong beliefs about the true consent required to create
a binding obligation, it escapes me how he could construe this to be a
voluntary compact. 'It remains only to be considered whether promises
extorted by force, without right, can be thought "consent", and how far
they bind. To which I shall say they bind not at all, because whatsoever
another gets from me by force I still retain the right of ... By the same
reason, he that forced a promise from me ought presently to restore it;
i.e., quit me of the obligations of it, or I may resume it myself; i.e., choose
whether I will perform it;' and, '... for what compact can be made with a
man that is not master of his own life? What condition can he perform?
And if he be once allowed to be master of his own life, the despotical
arbitrary power of his master ceases. He that is master of himself and his
own life has a right, too, to the means of preserving it; so that, as soon as
compact enters, slavery ceases.'[18]

The consent necessary to create a binding compact can be given only
by those who are in control, who are *masters*, of their own lives. But what
of women with child? Given the belief, false though it may be, that
women cannot on their own provide for their offspring, how could he
have believed them to be in a position to make the kind of contract which
he himself believed to be necessary to create binding obligations? Such
contracts, flowing from voluntary agreement, can be made only between
equals, where both parties bargain from positions of equal strength. But
how, in such circumstances, could women not be bargaining from a
position of weakness? And if the promise of the mother is extracted
under threat that unless she makes it, she will not have that required
support for their offspring, regardless of the fact that it may be her
natural right, then in what sense does this create a binding promise? It is
surely the sort of thing which someone with even an elementary knowledge of contract theory would know to fall dangerously close, if not well
within, the bounds of an unconscionable transaction.

However, leaving aside this issue, it is to Locke's credit that he saw
even the possibility of contractual marriage, which at least opens up the
possibility of a co-equal relationship between husband and wife. In para-
graph 83 of the *Second Treatise* he even goes so far as to suggest that the
absolute authority of husband over wife is not in fact necessary to the
chief end of marriage, namely, procreation, and, therefore, that marriage
'might be varied and regulated by that Contract, which unites Man and

Wife.'[19] Note, he does not say that it *ought* to be regulated by a contract which establishes a mutual authority, merely that it *might* be since this is not incompatible with the reproduction and rearing of children.

Unfortunately, however, Locke fails to mention that procreation is at most only one of the objectives of marriage, and while equality of husband and wife may be compatible with this function, it is incompatible with what he assumes to be the major function of marriage: to provide the mechanism for the transfer of property across generations. Locke may have tried to maintain that marriage is a voluntary contractual arrangement, which might even be varied to wrest absolute authority from the hands of the husband. Still, however, the husband had a power over his wife that she did not have over him. In the final analysis he is the ruler because he, and he alone, has the exclusive ability to control and to dispose of property. This was certainly the case under the marriage 'contracts' with which Locke was familiar and is indeed assumed throughout his own discussion. One of Locke's major objectives was to provide the theoretical basis for the absolute right of the male to pass his property to his rightful heirs. Clearly any variation in marriage contracts which moved toward any real equality between husband and wife would have to include an equal right to the disposition of family property; and this is obviously incompatible with Locke's objective of legitimizing exclusive male control of inheritable property.

Throughout the *Second Treatise* Locke always refers to family property as 'his' property, even though, for other purposes, he is at pains to show that the wife has a legitimate share in 'his' property. She has a right to a share of his property before and exclusive of strangers, namely, those who are not party to the marriage contract. Locke, in fact, makes a great deal of this, but not to ensure the equality of women either in or out of marriage. Rather he seeks to ensure that no absolute monarch, tyrant, conqueror, or usurper could alienate the male's property from his legitimate heirs. Locke says anything, advances any argument he can lay his hands on, to establish the principle that a man's legitimate heirs have a right to inherit his property, regardless even of the father's transgressions. So concerned is Locke to ensure the certainty and legitimacy of inheritance that he will allow even a wife a rightful share in property, but only *as against strangers*.

Locke is not concerned to ensure that either a wife or a man's children will inherit – that is, that they have a *right* to inherit which can be enforced against the husband/father. Whether or not they are to inherit depends on the arbitrary will of the male. Locke's point is to ensure that no government can have the right to dispossess a man eternally of his rightful property. He is not at all concerned to lay the basis for inheritance rights of the wife and heirs against the husband/father, but rather to lay as firm a foundation as possible for the right of wives and heirs to inherit to the exclusion of all others. This is not simply to ensure that his dependents are taken care of, but to establish the integrity of the male right to absolute dominion over the use and future disposition of his private property.

In 'Of Paternal Power' Locke clearly assumes the exclusive right of the male to dispose of familial property. So far as is consistent with fulfilling his obligation to provide support for his offspring, his right to dispose of his property is unlimited: 'a father may dispose of his own possessions as he pleases when his children are out of danger of perishing for want ... there is another power ordinary in the father whereby he has a tie on the obedience of his children; which, though it be common to him with other men, yet, the occasions of showing it almost constantly happening to fathers in their private families, and the instances of it elsewhere being rare and less taken notice of, it passes in the world for a part of paternal jurisdiction. And this is the power men generally have to bestow their estates on those who please them best; the possession of the father being the expectation and inheritance of the children, ordinarily in certain proportions according to the law and custom of each country, yet it is commonly in the father's power to bestow it with a more sparing or liberal hand, according as the behaviour of this or that child has comported with his will and humor.'[20]

In the passage cited earlier (page 19) in which he gives ultimate rule to husband over wife, by dint of his being naturally abler and stronger, he says that this does not give him dominion over what 'by contract is her peculiar right,' which sounds marvellously egalitarian, but what is more important is that it *does* extend to 'the things of their common interest and *property*'[21] (my emphasis). He makes it sound as if this is a limitation of male prerogative, when in fact it is just the reverse. By what earthly, or even heavenly, principles of fairness should she be entitled, on dissolution of the marriage contract, only to what she brought with her into it? Even this she would get only if she had been clever enough to get it covered in the contract and he had been willing to accept the contract on those terms.

Besides, as Locke well knew, the customs of his own country certainly did not allow women any control over the disposition of property, whether they owned it previously as *feme sole* (a woman without a husband), or acquired it after marriage. The situation up to 1882 and the passing of the first *Married Woman's Property Act*, is well summed up by Megarry: 'the wife had no power to dispose of her property *inter vivos*, and even with her husband's concurrence, had no power of disposition by will. The husband acting by himself, could dispose of an estate for his own lifetime, but no longer ... Leaseholds vested in the husband alone, and he could dispose of them in his lifetime without the concurrence of his wife. He could not, however, dispose of them by will, and on his death the wife's rights revived ... Pure personality vested in the husband absolutely and passed under any disposition by him whether *inter vivos* or by will, or on his intestacy.'[22]

Thus, the husband certainly had the real power. One might well ask what woman in her right mind would marry unless she had to, given her dependent status once she did. The idea that they were in any way mistresses of their own destiny and so in a position to bargain from positions of equality is surely a fiction of the first order. At least Locke suggests that the husband has some sort of moral, natural, duty to provide for his dependants, which, presumably, he would have been willing to see incorporated into the property laws for which his civil society was needed. This is something of an advance on the situation as it existed in England at the time, where, again to quote Megarry, 'From the Fourteenth century to 1939 there was in general no restriction upon a testator's power to dispose of property as he thought fit: for good reasons or bad, he might give all his property to a mistress or to charities and leave his family penniless.' Even on intestacy of the male the wife had no rights of inheritance at all, except those minor ones of dower: 'the issue were preferred to other relatives, the male issue being preferred to the female issue.'[23] But this is scant remedy for the clear injustices of the existing situation, and there is nothing in Locke to suggest that he thought his theory necessitated any sweeping changes in this particular respect.

This is all the more paradoxical in view of the fact that Locke believed marriage to be as much a fact of life in the state of nature as in civil society. The moral obligation to honour one's parents exists, says Locke, whether the child lives still under 'the law of nature or municipal law of their country.'[24] But more importantly, reproduction has no, and ought not to have any, civil consequences. The law, says Locke, has no right to make laws respecting filial duty. The husband/father rules in the family by dint of that 'executive power of the law of nature which every free man naturally has,' 'by virtue of that executive power of the law of nature which, as a man, he had a right to'; men are 'the natural fathers of families.' And the grouping of man and wife, which gave rise to parents and children, and even to master and servant, still 'came short of political society.'[25] Thus, all of this takes place in the state of nature and ought to remain unchanged in civil society, despite Locke's suggestion that it might be arranged otherwise.

But how could it in fact be changed and still preserve the function the family had of ensuring inheritance under control of the husband/father? Locke says nothing about the effects different marriage contracts would have on the distribution of family property. In fact, he does not acknowledge that this is in fact even one, much less the primary, objective of marriage law. Until well into the eighteenth century, the chief function of marriage was the preservation of family property across generations, and the formality of an actual marriage ceremony was, on the whole, reserved for the propertied classes. One's choice of a marriage partner was dictated by the demands of interest, not affection, and what held it together were considerations of property and lineage.[26] Property passed through blood lines and blood lines were determined by the father. Thus the authority of the father was essential in order to facilitate the regulation of property distribution within the framework Locke envisions.

As we have seen, Locke sees marriage as a natural association which occurs in the state of nature. But he says nothing whatsoever about how the authority of the husband over family property occurs in the state of nature, tracing, as he does, the formation of the family only in terms of its procreative function. Thus he provides no explicit explanation of why family property is under the control of the husband/father; but that it is so is certainly implicit throughout his argument. And though he appears to deny that the inequality of marriage must necessarily continue in civil society, it is clear that it must if property is to remain under the control of the husband/father. Marriage is already assumed at the point at which civil society begins, and so also is patriarchal control of family property.

It is highly significant that Locke discusses the possibility of marriage contracts based on mutual equality only in relation to the rearing of children and says not a word about this in relation to the distribution of property. The reason he did not is clear. Equality in marriage is not compatible with a system of property distribution accomplished through blood lines determined by the father. The exclusive male 'right' to dispose of family property can be established and maintained only by inequality in marriage at least concerning property. And surely no one would be inclined to argue that there is true equality in the marriage contract unless it applies to the right to control and dispose of property as well as to authority over children. Indeed, what could equal authority over children amount to unless it entailed the equal right of mother and father to determine the inheritance of each of the children? Thus, for Locke, the inequality of property between husband and wife is as firmly rooted in the state of nature and is as necessary within civil society as is the inequality of property between one man and another.

The inequality of power with respect to the control of property was not a product of civil society and could not be changed in civil society without disrupting the 'natural' method of property transfer accomplished by means of traditional marriage in which absolute authority over the disposition of property was vested in the husband alone. And that this authority should continue is assumed throughout Locke's argument. The inequality in the distribution of property between one man and another is, as we know, justified by reference to the greater industry and rationality of some men. For this reason the resulting unequal distribution should be protected by means of the coercive resources of civil society. But what could possibly justify the inequality between husband and wife in control and disposition of familial property? This is not even mentioned. Yet are not women as able to labour as men? Why ought not they to have a right to the products of their labour, and to that with which they have mixed their labour?

The question of the right of women to the products of their labour is mentioned only once. In 'Of Conquest' Locke settles in to establish that no monarch has the right to alienate eternally a man's private property, even when that man has acted on the side of injustice: 'Let the conqueror have as much justice on his side as could be supposed, he has no right to seize more than the vanquished could forfeit; his life is at the victor's mercy, and his service and goods he may appropriate to make himself reparation; but he cannot take the goods of his wife and children; they, too, had a title to the goods he enjoyed, and their shares in the estate he possessed ... I am conquered; my life, it is true, as forfeit, is at mercy, but not my wife's and children's. They made not the war nor assisted in it. I could not forfeit their lives; they were not mine to forfeit. My wife had a share in my estate; that neither could I forfeit. And my children also, being born of me, had a right to be maintained out of my labor or substance. Here then is the case: the conqueror has a title to reparation for damages received, and the children have a title to their father's estate for their subsistence.' He then goes on in the same passage to remark 'For as to the wife's share, whether her own labour or compact gave her title to it, it is plain her husband could not forfeit what was hers.'[27]

From this one can certainly conclude that woman's labour gives her title to possession. We have already seen that on dissolution of a marriage she was able to regain control of what she brought into the marriage by compact. But does she automatically retain control, by means of the marriage contract, over those things she has previously come to own by means of her labour? Does she have a claim to all things she gains by means of her labour during the marriage? If labour gives absolute title, why should it have to be further protected by means of an explicit contract? Most pressing of all, if she has absolute title through labour, by what principle does the husband gain control over her property *whether there is a contract or not*? And why should not her labour during marriage give her equal title to control, whether *inter vivos* or by testament, over their joint holdings?

Even if it can be argued that women, like men, are, in the state of nature, at liberty to appropriate and come to own property, how is it that they come to lose it by marriage, and why is it that during marriage their right to the product of their labour is extinguished? None of these questions are, of course, discussed, much less answered, by Locke. He simply assumes the status quo with respect to the property rights of married women and the dependent status for women that marriage creates. But what natural principles could possibly be advanced for this, since this is a situation which arises in the state of nature and must continue unchanged in civil society?

The answer, I suggest, is only too obvious. Because women are less able, and are weaker than men, they either do not appropriate, or, even if they do, have no claim to ownership. They are naturally inferior because weaker than men and are, therefore, naturally subject to their dominion. Even the arguments advanced for their rights vis-à-vis strangers are rights which *revive* when their husbands do something by which they forfeit some measure of their rights. Thus, the best light that can be put on things is that women's rights are dependent on men's rights. They do not have independent rights, and the reason for this is that they could not be regarded as independent persons with full property rights if the exclusive right of the male to dispose of property is to be maintained. They are not men and hence are not under the law of nature with respect to their equal right to be free of the dominion of any other person. That is assumed at the outset and is never challenged.

It is not to the point to argue in Locke's defence that it would be too much to expect him to challenge the existing status quo with respect to property and ownership within marriage. Locke was quite prepared to challenge the deepest principles of English land law, and, indeed, he did so.[28] But so far as the rights of women were concerned, he said not a word. He leaves them in the family, born in the state of nature and necessarily left unchanged in civil society, for even their rights as against strangers are grounded in the alleged natural law and principles applying to the state of nature. Thus he clearly accepted the premiss that there is a natural inequality between the sexes and that the male is by nature superior. He does not allow the reproductive function any place in political life; indeed, the facts of reproduction create no more rights or duties in civil society than exist in the state of nature with respect either to women or to children. Certainly no value is attached to reproduction even as part of that which gives significance to life for man. At best it is regarded as a natural inevitability which creates natural obligations for men, with respect both to support of their offspring and continued cohabitation with their wives.

There is, of course, an implicit significance for men in the conjugal relation which Locke regards as 'natural.' While he explains monogamy on the basis of the need for continued support of human offspring, and the natural obligation of human males to accept responsibility for the offspring they help to create, it is obvious that only monogamy ensures control over certainty of paternity. Only if a man controls a woman can he be sure that her offspring are equally his. This is deeply significant for Locke because of the value he attaches to private property and the absolute natural right a man has to pass his rightful property on to his legitimate heirs. While he did not want this natural right to account for the creation of government, since that would further serve the interests of patriarchal theories of government, that there was such a natural right is never questioned: 'All which are so many testimonies against paternal sovereignty, and plainly prove that it was not the natural right of the father descending to his heirs that made governments in the beginning, since it was impossible, upon that ground, there should have been so many little kingdoms.'[29] If significance for man is achieved through embodying himself in property which can persist through time, this significance can be achieved only if he can also ensure that those to whom such property passes are also 'his.' Thus certainty of paternity is as important for a significant life for man as is control of the future disposition of private property.[30]

In regarding marriage as he does, Locke is clearly making the relation between men and women subservient to the needs of ensured certainty of ownership under male control. The whole point of the theory is to guarantee absolute male ownership of private property, determinable over time. His limited discussion of marriage and of the relation between parents and children focuses only on the need for such relations because of the need for continuation of the species. It is a right to each other's bodies, about as materialistic as one can get. In discussing the relation of parents and children he stresses only the responsibilities the parental role imposes, its necessity in order to ensure that sons will grow up property tutored, their reason sufficiently developed to enable them to take over, and to exercise responsibly, the rights and duties of ownership.

The interesting point is that Locke's view of marriage as essentially instituted to preserve lineage is a precise articulation of the function marriage had at least up to the eighteenth century. Thus Locke is, here as elsewhere, defending the status quo: he is endorsing a view of marriage which sees it primarily as a mechanism for regulating the distribution of property along blood lines determined by the father. But it is significant that he does not articulate this as its function, but holds instead that it is a necessary institution because of the need for continuation of the species. He never even hints that it isn't continuity of the *species* which is important but ensured continuity of *individual* male heirs capable of functioning as the determinate future individuals on whom property held by individual men may devolve.

If one simply takes him at his word, and sees him as promulgating the view that marriage *ought* to be centrally concerned with the relations between husband and wife and between parents and children, where the rearing of children ought to be the real focus and purpose of marriage, one could see him as paving the way for modern-style 'companionate' marriage which began to emerge all across western Europe during the eighteenth century.[31] But it is impossible to see in him the precursor of a more 'liberal' attitude toward marriage and the relation of the sexes because he clearly endorsed the view that patriarchal control of family property ought to continue in civil society, and he consistently made the procreative responsibilities of marriage subservient to the needs of a system of individually held private property under the exclusive control of male 'heads of households.'

It isn't just that he assumed that this method of property disposition would continue, which could perhaps be explained by his failure of imagination with respect to alternative methods of property transfer across generations. His theory had two major objectives, the legitimizing of inequality in the distribution of property between one man and another (or, more accurately, as between one family and another), and the legitimizing of an exclusive male right to control and dispose of familial property. Thus it isn't simply that he thought patriarchal control of family property was the only available mechanism for ensuring the determination of property over time, but that it was in fact the only possible mechanism for ensuring one of his theoretical objectives.

Thus marriage and parenthood are not, for Locke, of intrinsic value. They are simply instrumental goods necessary for ensured male ownership of property over time. But even though, according to Locke, nothing but bare obligation, mutual right, holds husband to wife, the arrangement can hardly be reckoned a bad bargain when one considers the benefits with respect to property that then accrue to him. He gets everything the wife owned when she came into it, unless she can get it expressly excluded by contract. But then the terms of the contract come into effect only if there is a dissolution of the marriage or indiscretion on the part of the husband, and he can claim her labour as his own during the time of the marriage. All that and companionship too.

I conclude, therefore, that Locke's theory does display, unequivocally, sexist assumptions. What remains now is to show that the sexism cannot be expunged while leaving the theory defensible. What consequences follow if we take what he says about the state of nature and civil society and assume that his ontology includes both males and females? First of all, there is no marriage in the state of nature and women retain control over that with which they have mixed their labour. Or, even if they do become parties to (unenforceable) marriage contracts, they retain control over whatever property they already have and will continue to have the right both to appropriate and to control the property of their future labour. Thus, men do not have exclusive right to the disposition of familial property. Children or anyone else will be able to inherit directly from the woman/mother.

But the serious consequence for the theory is over the issue of control over the means and products of *reproduction*, of reproductive, rather than productive, labour. Who owns the children? If women are independently able to provide for themselves because they have the right to garner and control property, why should they care whose children they have, and why will it matter? And since children are the products of women's unique labour of reproduction, surely they alone are entitled to own them (assuming, of course, that anyone should). What reason will women have to ensure any particular man that the child they bear is his as well as theirs? And if anything does depend on it, how will the man be able to ensure that the child she says is his is really so? And without the certainty of paternity, what about the certainty of inheritance?

In the final analysis, what point is there to a theory whose sole object is to ensure the individual right of men to appropriate, own, and control the future disposition of property if they cannot be sure of the paternity of their potential inheritors? The theory which has this objective is inherently sexist because the chief end of it can be achieved only by keeping women in an inferior and dependent position in order to ensure certainty of paternity, and, hence, certainty of inheritance. Exclusively male control of the means and products of productive labour requires control of the means and products of reproductive labour. Thus, in so far as the peace, safety, and public good of the people consists in protecting the private property of individual men, then ownership of the means and products of reproduction is as necessary for this end as is protected ownership of the means and products of productive labour.

Locke appears to argue that because most women will be in need of support as a result of their biological liability with respect to reproduction, most women will therefore be married and hence subject to the will and authority of their husbands. The real argument, however, is that women's unique capacities with respect to reproduction *must be transformed into economic and social disadvantages* in order to ensure that they will be forced into a position of dependence on men. Thus, a system of private property owned and controlled by males necessitates transforming a mere biological difference into an economic and social disadvantage in order to ensure the continuation of that system.

Locke's theory is fundamentally sexist because it must treat a biological, 'natural,' difference between the sexes as a source of 'natural' inequality which licenses enshrining it as an economic and social disadvantage. Within Locke's theory women must *necessarily* be regarded as naturally disadvantaged. For unless they are so placed, they need not be dependent on men. And if they are not dependent on men, men would be unable to be sole owners of private property and would have no determinable heirs on whom to devolve the accumulated fruits of their labours.

Thus, the corner-stone of Locke's theory is an assumed natural disadvantage of women, and the ultimate objection to his theory is that it must convert a biological difference between the sexes into a socioeconomic liability. There is absolutely no reason why the biological difference between the sexes with respect to reproduction need lead to an inferior and dependent status for women. Indeed, this is acknowledged by Locke himself in allowing that women of means are not subject to the will and authority of their husbands. The difference between the sexes with respect to their role in relation to reproduction is no more a 'natural' disadvantage than is any other difference between persons. That it is a disadvantage is a result of convention and not nature.

Thus, in arguing against its being the product of law or convention, Locke's theory is, in the end, far more objectionable than that of Filmer, for Locke must insist on the natural inferiority of women due to their naturally disadvantaged position with respect to reproduction, while it is quite clear that that disadvantaged position can be brought about only by denying women access to the ownership and control of private property and thereby gaining the means to ensure their own survival and that of any children they might bear.

That the female role in relation to reproduction is a socio-economic disadvantage is obvious. But that it is a purely social disadvantage, a liability created not by 'nature' but by convention, is nowhere acknowledged by Locke, and indeed must be denied by him in order to generate the society he believes to be the only justifiable one. Since he says over and over again that the chief end of government is the protection of private property, and since it is assumed throughout that ownership and control of that property is in the hands of individual men, the conclusion I have advanced is unavoidable. To assume that women as well as men, whether married or single, could own and control property independently of men would destroy the allegedly natural domination of husband over wife and would destroy the necessity of a protected right to property disposition since it would lead to uncertainty of paternity.

Thus women's reproductive capacity must be embedded within a system of conventions whereby it creates an economic dependence, and that can be accomplished only by denying women rights to ownership and control of property as a consequence of their reproductive function. Locke's argument is basically very simple. The role of women is to bear men's children; the price of bearing children is loss of autonomy with respect to the acquisition, ownership, and control of property. Thus, women who bear children are and must be dependent on men for their survival and for the survival of their offspring. But, as is clear, there is absolutely no reason why reproduction should negate rights of ownership, indeed no reason why it should not generate such rights. What is just as clear, however, is that it must necessarily negate any such rights if the system is to be maintained in which men alone have the ability to accummulate forms of private property other than women and children. If Adam does not own Eve, how can he be sure who his descendants are, and, hence, on whom his apples ought properly to devolve? And if Eve owns her own apples, why should she obey Adam?

NOTES AND REFERENCES

This article is reprinted from *The Canadian Journal of Philosophy* vii (1977) 699–724 with the permission of the Canadian Association for Publishing in Philosophy.

1 See Lorenne Clark 'Rights of Women' in J. King-Farlow and W. Shea eds *Contemporary Issues in Political Philosophy* (New York 1976) 49–65.
2 Locke *Two Treatises of Government* ed Peter Laslett (New York 1963) 131
3 Ibid 47
4 Ibid 44
5 Ibid 47
6 Ibid 49, and see also 49: '... this Text gave not Adam that Absolute *Monarchical Power* our A[uthor, Filmer] Supposes ... but the Subjection of Eve to Adam, a Wife to her Husband.'
7 Ibid 54
8 He is singularly silent, however, on the issue of whether these are 'natural' differences. Given the things he cites, it hardly seems possible to construe all of them as in any way 'natural.' Thus, the differences between individual women, which can compensate for their 'natural' disadvantage, are likewise social and not natural.
9 *Treatises* 82
10 See Hobbes *Leviathan* chapter 20, and *Treatises* 364n.
11 *Treatises* 79-80
12 Ibid 105
13 At the heart of traditional political theory's inability to devise a theory which guarantees sexual equality is the assumption that women's unique capacities with respect to reproduction are natural, rather than social or conventional, disadvantages. Reproduction is consistently regarded as a natural *liability*. The point of the present paper is to show the centrality and necessity of this assumption within Locke's theoretical perspective.

14 I am much indebted to Professor John King-Farlow for many helpful comments he made on an earlier draft of this paper, particularly with respect to the conditions under which women's 'natural' inferiority may be overcome.

15 The most notable treatment is in C.B. Macpherson *The Political Theory of Possessive Individualism* (Oxford 1962). My own work has been greatly influenced by his views. Macpherson sees Locke as beginning from certain assumptions, which he designates 'natural,' which he then uses to justify gross inequality, when the reality of the case is that he must arrange social affairs to create the allegedly 'natural' state of affairs which is in fact necessary to bring about the state of inequality which he considers desirable.

16 *Treatises* 52. The quotations which follow in this section are from *Second Treatise* chapter 4, unless otherwise stated.

17 *Treatises* 2

18 Ibid 186 and 172

19 Ibid 83

20 Ibid 65, 72

21 Ibid 82

22 R.E. Megarry *A Manual of the Law of Real Property* 2nd ed (London 1955) 538

23 Ibid 291, 316. The dower rights of a widow entitled her to a life-estate in one-third of her husband's estate, whereas the courtesy rights of the widower entitled him to a life-estate in the whole of the real property of his deceased wife. (Women in England were worse off than black men in America: while black men were declared to be 3/5 of a white man, English women were clearly only 1/3 of an English man.)

24 *Treatises* 66

25 Ibid 70, 74, 76, 77

26 Edward Shorter *The Making of the Modern Family* (New York 1975), chs. 2 and 6 particularly

27 *Treatises* 183

28 The basis of English land law from the Norman conquest on was that all land was owned by the Crown, and was held by individuals only on sufferance. By the seventeenth century, this principle was, of course, being eroded. For all practical purposes, land was owned by individuals, in the sense that it was individuals who had exclusive right to the disposition of property they held, at least under some forms of holding. But the legal principle continued, and, indeed, continues to the present. Legally speaking, all land is held by the Crown. Locke attacked that fundamental con-

ception of the basis of English land law at its very root in arguing that the land was given by God to all men in common. He is thus attempting to provide an alternative basis of individual rights of ownership, and to trace rights of ownership from God rather than from the Monarch. No doubt it was his strong desire to wrest rights with respect to land away from the monarchy which lies at the heart of his strong distaste for monarchy.

29 *Treatises* 115

30 The idea that the certainty of paternity and the need for continuity through time are basic issues motivating the direction of Western political theory is discussed and developed by Mary O'Brien in 'The Politics of Impotence' in King-Farlow and Shea eds *Contemporary Issues in Political Philosophy*. The issue of the relation between control of the means and products of production and control of the means and products of reproduction is discussed further in 'Politics and Law.'

31 Shorter *Modern Family* 227

Rousseau:
Women and the General Will

LYNDA LANGE

The work of Jean-Jacques Rousseau is the first major attempt to justify equality among men. His work also contains a justification of the *in*-equality of men and women, and an elaborate treatment of their respective 'natures' as he saw them.

From the perspective of feminist scholarship, this presents an interesting study, for several reasons. The first is the familiarity to the modern reader of Rousseau's ideas about women, which argues for their influence, or at the very least their timeliness. Unlike such works as Aristotle's closely reasoned biological and philosophical treatment of sex difference, or the virtual vilification of women by nineteenth-century writers such as Schopenhauer or Nietszche, Rousseau's ideas about women are readily comprehensible to us. *Émile*, his treatise on education, contains a full treatment of the subject. It was a very influential work, sometimes credited with the virtual invention of the modern Western romantic concept of childhood as a state of innocent pleasures from which we are reluctantly expelled at maturity. Also an invention of the early modern period, and espoused by Rousseau, is the correlated necessity for the constant care of a devoted biological mother, and the romantic, male-dominant, view of marriage.[1]

The second reason is the persistence of the view that sexual role differentiation, and accompanying ideas about differences in female and male 'natures,' do not necessarily represent sexism, or perpetuate the oppression of women.[2] This interpretation may be particularly tempting in the case of Rousseau because of his reputation as a defender of equality. He makes a pretence of holding this view himself. He writes, 'A perfect man and a perfect women should no more be alike in mind than in face, and perfection admits of neither less nor more.'[3] This approach may be at present the most common defence of such views by those who espouse them while not wishing to be considered sexist. I shall examine the logical structure of this approach, in order to assess whether or not such a view can be defended in the case of Rousseau.

The third reason for examining Rousseau applies to the work of all political philosophers who have offered theories about the roles of the sexes and the form of the family. These views are now considered doubtful enough that few would willingly correlate the interest or correctness of the historically influential political theories with the interest or correctness of their accompanying theories of sex difference. Recent scholars and educators have for the most part ignored the latter theories, on the assumption that they do not materially affect the status of the rest of the theory. Whether or not this approach is sound is a question which I believe ought to be asked about every political system that is not explicitly egalitarian regarding the sexes. In the case of Rousseau, the crux of the matter is whether or not the 'general will' is a concept that could be made genuinely egalitarian, i.e. is it plausible that all adults, women and men, could be associates of the general will? I shall argue that it is not, and that the insistence on sexual equality exposes the weaknesses of the concept of the general will in an illuminating way.

The view that sexual role differentiation is not *necessarily* oppressive is no doubt true, strictly speaking. A belief that the sexes are, or ought to be, different in social role and/or 'nature' does not in itself *imply* that the difference will include an unequal distribution of power, or the exploitation of one sex by the other. But suppose for the sake of argument that one wanted to justify a 'different but equal' set of sexual roles; what would be required for such a justification? I shall suggest an answer to this question, and on the basis of it, go on to ask whether or not Rousseau's view of sexual roles can be made to fit this model.

To begin with, I intend to discuss sexual roles in the sense of *social* roles – roles played within a human society, and therefore having meaning only in this context. The significance of such a role may, therefore, only be understood by awareness not only of the things associated with it, but also of the things it excludes.

A social role may be thought to involve many things, from type of work, through specialized aptitudes and skills, to general temperament, manners, dress, use of language, and so on. Certainly all of these things are relevant when examining sexual role differentiation as we know it. But they are not all equally crucial, since some are basic and others are consequences of the basic difference. My hypothesis is that the crux of a social role played by a substantial portion of the population is always the useful social function that persons playing that role perform as a group. If this is correct, the existence of the role should be discovered on analysis to have a useful material function for the society in question.

The 'female role' fits this hypothesis extremely well, for the basis of it in all societies appears to be the performance of a very useful function indeed, what I call 'reproductive labour.' 'Reproductive labour' is distinct in concept from biological reproduction, and refers specifically to the adult expenditure of time and effort in the provision of nurture and active socialization to physically dependent children. I maintain elsewhere that the performance of this labour is at the bottom of all the non-biological differences between the sexes.[4] It is apparent, of course, that reproductive labour, as I have defined it, *may* be done by both sexes.[5]

On this hypothesis about sexual roles we should expect that a justification of different roles for the sexes will be based ultimately on their supposed fitness for certain important catagories of tasks. It will be shown that Rousseau attempts to justify his views on this basis. In view of Rousseau's egalitarianism, and his notorious championship of 'the natural,' it is further to be expected in his case that he would consider the difference in sexual roles to be 'natural,' and this too will be shown.

The sexual division of labour, according to Rousseau, is a state of affairs that is unquestionably pre-political, though interestingly enough, not really pre-social. One might well wonder how it could possibly be pre-*social*, requiring as it does an association of some sort, yet in the history of theory the existence of a biological, patriarchal, family is often treated as pre-social in the sense of being prior to human society and part of 'brute nature.' Rousseau's state of nature differs from that of both Thomas Hobbes and John Locke, in that 'the individual' is *not* originally conceived of as 'the male head of a family.' Rousseau's 'natural man' is a totally independent individual who immediately gratifies whatever sexual desire presents itself to consciousness when he happens to encounter a female, and is otherwise little troubled by sexual need.[6] It is noteworthy, of course, that this is conceived of from a strictly masculine point of view.

Nevertheless, the patriarchal family does not appear at the dawn of time, according to Rousseau, but at the dawn of what may properly be called human history, at about the same time that language first makes an appearance. Prior to that, males and females filled their material, if not their sexual, needs with exactly the same activities. According to Rousseau, the building of huts appeared as a new skill, and resulted in the establishment of families consisting of biological parents and their offspring. Rousseau assumes that this resulted automatically in a sexual division of labour. 'The sexes,' he writes, 'whose manner of life had been hitherto the same, began now to adopt different ways of living. The women became more sedentary, and accustomed themselves to mind the hut and their children, while the men went abroad in search of their common subsistence.'[7] That the crux of the sexual difference is different sets of necessary social tasks is already quite clear.

This is speculative history, however, and I am concerned with the logic of justification, by which I mean morally acceptable justification. Such a history may, of course, function as a justification of sorts in some theoretical contexts, but Rousseau also provides other justification. Eighteenth-century Europe was full of inequality, and Rousseau was the first major thinker to provide a theory which was critical of existing male inequality. It may be because he makes fewer assumptions than others about the timelessness of the patriarchal family, and about social inequality in general, that he is forced to go farther in the process of justifying the one form of inequality he wishes to defend. Where other thinkers may provide only arguments about the pragmatic value of patriarchal authority, Rousseau adds to that a difference between the sexes in God-given essence! In *Émile* he writes: '[God] has endowed man with boundless passions ... though swayed by these passions man is endowed with reason by which to control them. Woman is also endowed with boundless passions; God has given her modesty to restrain them.'[8] In the ensuing process of arguing that child-bearing and rearing are the 'proper business' of women, he argues that the requirements for it are incompatible with those of masculine occupations. He writes: 'Can she be a nursing mother to-day and a soldier tomorrow? Will she change her tastes and her feelings as a chameleon changes his colour? Will she pass at once from the privacy of household duties and indoor occupations to the buffeting of the winds, the toils, the labours, the perils of war?'[9]

While not denying the potential effects of education, he argues that women are naturally weak, 'passive,' and 'timid,'[10] and that these qualities are actually useful for the performance of their special duties and for their preservation in a role that requires dependence on men. He writes: 'She cannot fulfill her purpose in life without his aid, without his good-will, without his respect; she is dependent on our feelings, on the price we put upon her virtue, etc;' and further: 'habitual restraint produces a docility which woman requires all her life long, for she will always be in subjection to a man, or to man's judgment ... she must be gentle for her own sake, not his. Bitterness and obstinacy only multiply the sufferings of the wife.'[11]

Thus there is both a descriptive and a prescriptive element in the theory. Not only is it the case that women have historically done the reproductive labour, according to Rousseau, but it is also the case that they are naturally fit for it, and therefore ought to do it. The role of citizen, on the other hand, is what men are fit for, Rousseau being the first great defender of universal male citizenship. What this role requires will be considered in the discussion of the general will.

Those who defend views such as the above as non-oppressive usually attempt to accomplish their task by offering a 'cleaned-up' version which eliminates the more pejorative terms in the description of the nature of women, and by such devices as replacing a phrase like 'obey your husband' with the current one, 'support your husband.' But such efforts do not alter the basic structure of the view. If such roles, or some modification of them, are different but *equal*, then neither role should carry with it a disproportionate sacrifice of opportunities for self-development within the norms of a given society. This means that an individual should not, as a consequence of playing the role, be deprived of such social values as full citizenship, economic independence, sense of self-worth supported by acknowledgment of worth by others, and so on.

The introduction of a device following the method of John Rawls[12] may help to clarify this point. Different but equal social roles may be defined as being such that they would be deemed to be equal by persons behind a veil of ignorance that includes ignorance of their sex.

I believe that the establishment of 'different but equal' status would involve four distinct claims. To begin with, let us assume that society requires the performance of two different types of task: the production of a subsistence for all members, and the reproduction of new individuals (including reproductive labour). While the resources allocated to these two tasks will vary, neither of them can be reduced below a quite substantial level.

Let x-tasks and y-tasks be these equally necessary, but different, types of task. Let s and p be groups of people large enough to correspond to these necessities; s and p taken together will probably comprise almost the whole of the adult population. The four claims may then be usefully thought of as having the following form:

1 Ss are best fit to do x-tasks
2 Ss are unfit to do y-tasks
3 Ps are best fit to do y-tasks
4 Ps are unfit to do x-tasks

	s		p	
	x-tasks	y-tasks	x-tasks	y-tasks
1	f	f	f	f
2	f	f	f	u
3	f	f	u	f
4	f	u	u	f
5	u	f	f	f
6	u	f	f	u
7	f	u	f	f

Nothing less than this will cover all possibilities. The table lists some possible combinations of fitness and unfitness (f = fit, u = unfit). Of the possibilities given here, there appear to be only seven interesting cases, since cases where s or p, or both, are unfit for both types of necessary social task are not useful here. Only two of the seven fit the above model (lines 4 and 6). For the remaining five, it is possible to show that they conflict with our ordinary ideas about what is fair in such matters. For example, where s and p are both fit for both x-tasks and y-tasks (line 1), there is, of course, no argument based on the 'natures' of persons of either sort, for role differentiation.

If s is fit for both x-tasks and y-tasks, but p is fit only for x-tasks (line 2), then it appears to be necessary for p to do x-tasks, and s to perform y-tasks. But since s is equally fit for x-tasks, this may not be s's preference. Hence exclusion from x-tasks may be unfair to s, if 'fitness for tasks' is our ostensible criterion. This argument is applicable to all of the remaining lines (3,5,7). An argument based on anything less than these four types of claim is not morally acceptable from an egalitarian point of view, and is most likely to turn out to be an argument from efficiency.

However, so long as these claims have the form indicated, and are perfectly symmetrical, they may possibly be considered as a justification of different but equal functions for groups of people in society. I shall show that in the case of Rousseau there are important asymmetries.

The ultimate character and significance of these asymmetries depends on the character of the general will, which is the core of Rousseau's theory of the ideal civil state. All citizens, according to Rousseau, must participate in the expression of the general will in the making of laws, or it simply is not the general will, but merely the particular will of some portion of society. 'Any formal exclusion,' he writes, 'is a breach of generality.'[13] It is clear that there is no basis in his theory for the exclusion of any who are, in virtue of their inborn 'nature' or faculties, fit to be associates of the general will.

The generality of the general will is not to be merely quantitative in terms of participation, however. The objects of this will are also general, that is, general laws which apply with equal force to everyone, so that no one is supposed to have any particular interests that might be served by any of the pronouncements of the general will. Equality of the associates is a necessary condition for this, since Rousseau argues that, where there is inequality 'laws are always of use to those who possess and harmful to those who have nothing.'[14] There is a further reason why the associates must be equal; this reason will emerge below. Each associate is to attempt to decide rationally and objectively what would be for the common good, hence the general will is distinct from, and transcends, the sum of particular wills and is not just a majority vote. Rationality is the essence of the general will, and the capacity for it is, so to speak, the individual's ticket for admission to the assembly of citizens.

We have examined briefly the role of women and their 'natural' fitness for that role, according to Rousseau. But what is Rousseau's view of the individual 'nature' of those who may be associates of the general will? The capacity for rationality has suggested to different thinkers a very wide variety of personal attributes. Though Rousseau is less than clear and systematic on this question, his writings on the subject do yield a few specific ideas, enough to make his concept of rationality distinctive. I believe that he had a notion of a uniquely human attribute that develops only in the civil society governed by the general will, and that he distinguished this from instrumental rationality, which may be used for good or bad ends in any society.

In the first place, citizenship requires the ability on the part of the individual to transcend personal, particular interests. The common good as determined by the general will may require the individual to accept real personal sacrifices. This distinguishes Rousseau's ideas completely from those of the Hobbesians, the Lockeans, and ideas of 'economic man' of all sorts. According to these systems, self-interest may only become enlightened and learn to take a long-range view of things – it may never be transcended. The transcendence required by Rousseau has two aspects. Self-mastery, according to the Greeks, and according to Rousseau, is a pre-condition for attainment in thought of the level of the universal. In *The Social Contract* Rousseau writes: 'add to what man acquires in the civil state, moral liberty, which alone makes him truly master of himself; for the mere impulse of appetite is slavery, while obedience to a law which we prescribe to ourselves is liberty.'[15]

The other quality that a bearer of Rousseau's highest form of rationality must have may be called independence or autonomy. Rousseau makes an important distinction between amour de soi, the healthy, noncomparative love of self, and amour propre, the self-conscious, relativistic concern for the opinions of others. The latter is the subjective state that accompanies inequality, since, according to Rousseau, inequality, not 'human nature,' is the source of the universal insecurity of a Hobbesian 'war of all against all.' Unlike Hobbes, however, Rousseau does not believe that this condition is the inevitable consequence of human nature unchecked by authority. According to him, it is just the reverse. In *A Discourse on the Origin of Inequality Among Men* Rousseau writes: 'Social man lives constantly outside himself, and only knows how to live in the opinion of others, so that he seems to receive the consciousness of his own existence merely from the judgment of others concerning him. It is not to my present purpose to insist on the indifference to good and evil which arises from this disposition ... this is not by any means the original state of man, but it is merely the spirit of society, and the inequality which society produces, that thus transform and alter all our natural inclinations.'[16] Inequality and the resultant amour propre present an insurmountable obstacle to the discovery of the general will, non-subjective as it is supposed to be, because they prevent the individual from making independent evaluative judgments.

I have aimed at two distinct conclusions. One is the claim that Rousseau's concept of citizenship cannot be universalized for all adults, women and men, even in theory. The other is that, even were we to suppose sexual roles necessary or desirable, Rousseau's arguments do not fit the model of 'different but equal' sexual-role differentiation which I presented earlier.

With regard to the question of universal citizenship, it is apparent that the social role of women as 'natural' reproductive workers is incompatible with participation in the general will. According to Rousseau, women are 'naturally' dependent on men for the fulfillment of their role, and as a consequence could not have the requisite autonomy of judgment. They must not only be confined to family life and excluded from public life, but also must be subservient to men *within* the private sphere itself. In the course of arguing that the father ought to command in the family, Rousseau writes: 'However lightly we may regard the disadvantages peculiar to women, yet, as they necessarily occasion intervals of inaction, this is a sufficient reason for excluding them from this supreme authority ... Besides, the husband ought to be able to superintend his wife's conduct, because it is of importance for him to be assured that the children, whom he is obliged to acknowledge and maintain, belong to no one but himself.'[17]

In the fifth book of *Émile* we find the moral differences between men and women elaborated in great detail, her moral status being defined completely in relation to men: 'Thus it is not enough that a woman should be faithful; her husband, along with his friends and neighbours, must believe in her fidelity ... Nature herself has decreed that women, both for herself and her children, should be at the mercy of man's judgment ... Worth alone will not suffice, a woman must be thought worthy; nor beauty, she must be admired; nor virtue, she must be respected ... "What will people think" is the grave of a man's virtue and the throne of a woman's.'[18] Rousseau is quite explicit about the 'natural' differences between the sexes that go with the differences between wife and citizen. In the fifth book of *Émile* he says: 'Woman is made to submit to man and to endure even injustice at his hands. You will never bring young lads to this: their feelings rise in revolt against injustice; nature has not fitted them to put up with it.'[19]

Now, as we have seen, Rousseau has forcefully argued that inequality, coupled with a lack of moral autonomy, is inimical to the formation of independent, non-subjective, judgments. Clearly, women could not be associates of the general will while performing their natural role as Rousseau has defined it. As a first attempt at eliminating the sexism of the theory of the general will, the patriarchal family would have to be eliminated. This is the step that modern students of the so-called 'main' theory, who do not consider the problem of sexism very deeply, may take for granted. But is such a modification feasible? I maintain it is not.

Rousseau makes an explicit philosophical distinction between the family (and other aspects of private life) and citizenship, or public life. The latter is associated with the sphere of generality, that is, of discourse and judgment about the loftiest of intentional objects and moral sentiments. The family is the sphere of the particular, of appetite, emotion, and sentiment. The dualism of mind and body which underlies this distinction has played a very important role in the history of political theory, where it is used as part of the philosophical foundation of the justification of hierarchical structures.

It is usually argued that those who best exercise the functions of mind are the ones who ought to rule those dominated by appetite or sentiment. The problem is then reduced to one of identifying these individuals. Since the material needs of society, along with the will and passions of its individual members, may never be dispensed with, however much they may be controlled or denigrated, the dualist must assign these activities to some segment of society. We have, for example, the artisan class in Plato's *Republic*, and the servant class in *The Second Treatise* of John Locke. 'Naturally', these stewards of the appetite need to be ruled by those who are stewards of something considered higher and better. Now Rousseau has made the radical claim that equality is essential for the rational governance of society for the 'common good.' But operating as he is from an extreme dualistic position, the accommodation of both aspects of human nature in society still requires a literal separation of function. The stewards of the appetite have all become stewardesses! – but no less essential to the body politic for all that.

In subjective terms, the nature of Rousseau's ideal state makes the refuge of the home a virtual necessity for the citizen. Because the demands of citizenship are so stringent and impersonal, it would be appalling to imagine everyone called to that status. At least Rousseau himself finds it appalling. In the course of arguing for the incompatibility of 'natural' feelings with ideal social life, in the first part of *Émile*, he writes: 'A Spartan mother had five sons with the army. A Helot arrived; trembling she asked his news. "Your five sons are slain." "Vile slave, was that what I asked thee?" "We have won the victory." She hastened to the temple to render thanks to the gods. That was a citizen.'[20] When citizens are like this, citizen mothers are evidently monsters.

Beyond our subjective impression, however, we may note that Rousseau is a notorious champion of 'natural' feeling, and defender of the importance of family life, in spite of, or I would say, more likely, because of, his rarefied view of citizenship.

He criticized what he calls the 'political promiscuity' of Plato's *Republic*, under which, he writes, 'the same occupations are assigned to both sexes alike, a scheme which could only lead to intolerable evils.' He explains this view as follows: 'I refer to that subversion of all the tenderest of our natural feelings, which he sacrificed to an artificial sentiment which can only exist by their aid. Will the bonds of convention hold firm without some foundation in nature? Can devotion to the state exist apart from the love of those near and dear to us? Can patriotism thrive except in the soil of that miniature fatherland, the home? Is it not the good son, the good husband, the good father, who makes the good citizen?'[21] The *Republic* is a work to which Rousseau is indebted in other respects. In both the *Republic* and *The Social Contract*, society is to be ruled for 'the common good' by means of the right use of wisdom and reason on the part of certain individuals. In neither case, however, is the conclusion drawn that this activity could be made universal for all adults. I maintain that the justification of different social and sexual roles for different people is always based on an emphasis on some aspect of human capability at the expense of the rest, with the insistence all the while, of course, that for each group the capacity essential for their role is dominant. It appears that a truly egalitarian political theory, without a hierarchy of social roles, must include a philosophy of synthesis or harmony of reason and appetite, not one of their opposition. Rousseau may have believed he accomplished this, because he believed that for egalitarianism it was sufficient to consider men. I believe, however, that my analysis shows the extent to which he was unsuccessful, precisely because he retained an inferior social group (women) as caretakers of the 'lesser' human needs of emotion and appetite.

In conclusion, Rousseau's justification of sexual roles fits the model wherein the roles in question are based on fitness for certain categories of tasks, one group considered on the whole fit for one category of tasks, and the other for another. The difficulty arises in that these tasks are not different in the way that, say, carpentry and farming are different. The categories of tasks, x and y, are different in that the putatively highest form of reason is necessary to do, say, x, but not to do y. This creates assymmetry in the four claims that are part of the model because those who are said to have this faculty of reason have it *in addition* to putatively lesser faculties, and not *instead of* them. Claim 2 is then distorted to mean, not that ss are unfit to do y because they are unable to do it well or at all, but 'unfit' because it would be a waste of their potential. So claim 2 is really a corollary of claim 1. Furthermore, claim 3 collapses into claim 4, since Ps are not ultimately best fit to do y on account of their ability for y, but on account of their lack of ability for x, which invariably turns out to be their lack of the specific sort of rationality. Claims 1 and 4 remain, their justification being sufficient for the justification of a hierarchical set of social roles, as opposed to an egalitarian one.

NOTES AND REFERENCES

1 See Edward Shorter *The Making of the Modern Family* (New York 1975) for the development of sentiment as the basis of family ties and the mother-child relationship, and the correlated increase in privacy.
2 See, for example, David Gauthier 'The Rationale of Differential Sexual Socialization' unpublished paper, University of Toronto, n.d. Gauthier

uses an argument from practical necessity. By contrast, E.B. Leacock, an anthropologist, argues that there have been societies organized by 'clan' wherein the only division of labour was by sex. She describes a situation in which the sexual division of labour was 'reciprocal,' rather than dependent/superior. She argues that since both sexes made important contributions to the livelihood of the group, *and* this fact was reflected in their social organization, the division into sexual roles was not oppressive: Leacock, Introduction to Engels *The Origin of the Family, Private Property, and the State* tr E.B. Leacock (New York 1973).

3 *Émile* tr B. Foxley (New York and London 1969) 322
4 Lynda Lange 'Reproduction in Democratic Theory' J. King-Farlow and W. Shea eds *Contemporary Issues in Political Philosophy* (New York 1976)
5 The concept of 'reproductive labour' helps to explain why it is somewhat easier for women to gain the privilege of such things as wearing pants, exercising sexual initiative, or even doing philosophy and driving trucks, than it is for them to *cease* changing diapers, staying home with the kids, cooking, and so on.
6 Rousseau 'A Discourse on the Origin of Inequality among Men' *The Social Contract and Discourses* tr G.D.H. Cole (London 1973) 70-2
7 Ibid 80
8 *Émile* 323
9 Ibid 325
10 Ibid 322, 326n
11 Ibid 328, 333
12 John Rawls *A Theory of Justice* (Cambridge, Mass. 1971)
13 *Social Contract and Discourses* 183n
14 Ibid 181n
15 Ibid 178
16 'Origin of Inequality' ibid 104-5
17 'A Discourse on Political Economy' ibid 118
18 *Émile* 325, 328. Rousseau's ostensible rationale for all of this is ultimately the need for the male head of a family to know that his children are his. The economic correlates of this are his responsibility for their support and his access to the means to do so, and the mother's corresponding lack of such access. This rationale is not in contradiction with the rationalization of the social role of women as reproductive workers. In fact, the reasonings are mutually reinforcing.
19 Ibid 359
20 Ibid 8
21 Ibid 326

Hume on Women

I *The Humean female*

STEVEN A. MACLEOD BURNS

Book I of *A Treatise of Human Nature* is, as Hume said it was, the real introduction to the book on morals.[1] Empiricism had triumphed in the natural sciences, and Hume intended to establish it as the basis of a naturalistic ethics, freed from rationalism and dogmatism.[2] This can be seen clearly enough from the way Hume constructed *An Enquiry Concerning the Principles of Morals.* The dominant claim is that there can be no answer to the controversy with which the discussion is opened – whether morality be derived from reason, from sentiment, from both, or from neither – without an empirical investigation of the subject.

An empirical investigation should: 'follow a very simple method: we shall analyse that complication of mental qualities, which form what, in common life, we call Personal Merit: we shall consider every attribute of the mind, which renders a man an object either of esteem and affection, or of hatred and contempt ... [The philosopher] needs only enter into his own breast for a moment, and consider whether or not he should desire to have this or that quality ascribed to him ... The very nature of language guides us almost infallibly in forming a judgement of this nature ... The only object of reasoning is to discover the circumstances on both sides, which are common to these qualities ... and thence to reach the foundation of ethics, and find those universal principles, from which all censure or approbation is ultimately derived. As this is a question of fact, not of abstract science, we can only expect success, by following the experimental method, and deducing general maxims from a comparison of particular instances.'[3]

This is Hume's new method in moral philosophy; he founds it on fact and observation. One might easily imagine, knowing that he 'took a particular pleasure in the company of modest women,' and knowing the general class of women he had in mind, that his observation would lead him to think of women as charming and intelligent, but as having power only in the salon, not in the world. This would not be far wrong. It should be remembered, however, that on at least one occasion Hume was involved with a woman whom he found so attractive and so fickle that he felt himself in danger.[4]

The actual product of his empirical search for a model of Personal Merit is an ideal male named Cleanthes, who is presented to us in the 'Conclusion' of the moral *Enquiry*. You are to imagine that you have given your daughter to him, and that other gentlemen congratulate you by describing your son-in-law as fair and humane, conscientious and skilful, witty and well-mannered, and cheerful and calm. These are, in order, qualities useful to others and to himself, and qualities immediately agreeable to others and to himself. Qualities under these four headings naturally strike us as attractive, and 'a philosopher might select this character as a model of perfect virtue.'[5]

The self-evidence of the virtuousness of Cleanthes is underlined by the equally self-evident unpleasantness of his foil, the 'gloomy, hair-brained enthusiast,' who has all the opposite qualities: 'Celibacy, fasting, penance, mortification, self-denial, humility, silence, solitude, and the whole train of monkish virtues ... [are] everywhere rejected by men of sense ... because they serve to no manner of purpose; neither advance a man's fortune in the world, nor render him a more valuable member of society; neither qualify him for the entertainment of company, nor increase his power of self-enjoyment. We observe, on the contrary, that they cross all these desirable ends ... We justly, therefore, transfer them to the opposite column, and place them in the catalogue of vices.'[6] Such a person might qualify for the calendar of saints, but not for any desirable marriage or civil-service post.

Hume presents his Cleanthes as a model human, not as a model male, but there are reasons for thinking that his model female would not only have different qualities, but would be distinctly inferior. For instance, Hume writes that modesty and chastity are duties 'which belong to the fair sex,' and that in this regard there is a 'vast difference' between the two sexes.[7] Chastity is not one of the natural virtues, but is 'artificial' or contrived for external reasons. Though not pleasant in itself, it is a virtue because it is conducive to certain ends the alternatives to which are decidedly disagreeable. These consequences tend to affect the female, not the male. For these reasons, what is scarcely a virtue at all in Cleanthes is the greatest one attainable by his female counterpart. 'The greatest regard, which can be acquired by that sex, is derived from their fidelity ... The smallest failure here is sufficient to blast her character.'[8]

If the obligations of the woman with regard to chastity are much greater than those of the man, this is because it is on her that the marks of failure (defloration and pregnancy) are most visibly displayed. Women must be trained in this virtue from an early age so that their minds will be set against any breach of the convention, and indeed so that they will be disposed to be wary of even the little pleasantries and intimacies which we call flirtation: 'A female has so many opportunities of secretly indulging these appetites, that nothing can give us security but her absolute modesty and reserve; and where a breach is once made, it can scarcely ever be fully repaired. If a man behave with cowardice on one occasion, a contrary conduct re-instates him in his character. But by what action can a woman, whose behaviour has once been dissolute, be able to assure us, that she has formed better resolutions, and has self-command enough to carry them into execution?'[9] It is clearly not Hume's intention that these be seen as recommendations, nor does he present them as conclusions of deductive moral reasoning; these are the observations of current practice, indeed of the 'practice and sentiments of all nations and ages', which he claims constitute his data. His theoretical aim is to show that moral and political conventions are founded on public interest, that they are useful to society.

In the present case, what needs explanation is the purpose of purity and self-denial. Hume is enigmatic: 'The long and helpless infancy of man requires the combination of parents for the subsistence of their young; and that combination requires the virtue of chastity or fidelity to the marriage bed. Without such a *utility*, it will readily be owned, that such a virtue would never have been thought of.'[10] What utility is this? In the chapter on chastity in the *Treatise*, he explains that it is the male's being able to identify a child as his own which is at stake. If a woman is subject to any suspicion about her chastity then there can be no certainty about the identity of her offspring's father. And of what importance is this? It is required of a man that if he father children he contribute to their nurture.

Spending money on others is by and large not a natural activity, but if the species is to survive the breadwinner must be moved to comply. This can be made to appear useful to him if it can be connected not with the expending of his material substance, but with the preservation of it through the establishment of heirs to his estate. But even this will not rouse his natural sentiments if the children are not themselves the products of the father: 'In order to induce the men to impose on themselves this restraint, and undergo chearfully all the fatigues and expences, to which it subjects them, they must believe, that the children are their own, and that their natural instinct is not directed to a wrong object ... Men are induc'd to labour for the maintenance and education of their children, by the persuasion that they are really their own; and therefore 'tis reasonable, and even necessary, to give them some security in this particular.'[11]

Thus to ensure that a child will be fed, a man must be assured that he was in fact responsible for its conception. A society has utilitarian reasons for insisting on female chastity. It might appear that it is not really the woman's problem. She knows the child is hers. It is the man who has the interest in knowing that a child is his; he should be the one to shoulder the corresponding obligations. This, however, overlooks not just the difficulty of distinguishing the males of 'blasted' character from the chaste ones, but more importantly the real burden of the female. The individual woman's interest is crucial. If she desires that her offspring be provided for, she will take pains to see that there is no doubt which male is responsible. In effect, by virtue of the male's economic power the female is condemned to chastity.

This treatment of chastity as a virtue primarily for women is sexist both in substance and in implication. It constitutes unjust discrimination between male and female. Not only does Hume think different qualities admirable in the different sexes, which is discriminatory, but the men get the benefit, and the women have to accept the harder, less pleasant virtue, which is not only discriminatory but unfair. 'Thus batchelors, however debauch'd, cannot chuse but be shock'd with any instance of lewdness or impudence in women.'[12] Further, the grounds on which this double standard is adopted, implying as they do that men are the possessors of both property and children, and the only providers of goods from the world outside the home, are themselves fundamentally sexist.

Let us now approach the subject from the political direction by considering the notions of justice, equality, and power. No raving democrat (though he called himself 'American in my principles' in a letter of 1775), Hume held no brief, either, for greater equality in wealth. Besides offering reasons in favour of some persons' having great riches, he argues vigorously against the economic egalitarianism promoted by the Levellers.

The arguments are instructive. There are four of them purporting to show the policy both impractical and (were it possible) pernicious: Either (1) Men of differing talents and virtues will upset the equality immediately; or (2) those talents will have to be suppressed and wasted, reducing all the people to indigence, and (3) such suppression will require extensive tyrannical powers. Hume has in mind a particular example. It is described in Hendel's summary of Hume's *History of England*: 'Then the Levellers, very radical in their aims to secure equal liberty for all, overturned the Army authority and also exercised arbitrary power. Oliver Cromwell could only check their unbounded license with another authority of his own as Protector, and so the history had come in a full circle to the rule of one man, as it was in the beginning.'[13]

Then, undermining his own case, Hume presents his fourth argument: '(4) Such extensive powers could not in such circumstances be assembled, for 'perfect equality of possessions, destroying all subordination, weakens extremely the authority of magistracy, and must reduce all power nearly to a level, as well as property.'[14]

We shall set aside the debatable presuppositions of these arguments (e.g. that carefulness produces wealth and that the wealth is the producer's; a counter-example to both claims is a parent careful with her infant), and look at the fourth argument in particular. It shows Hume expecting that disparities of wealth (including 'want and beggary in a few') are necessary to sustain the power which makes subordination to authority, and thus government, possible. He does not, of course, espouse absolute authority and total submission, and a certain degree of equality is requisite for human society – but one mustn't have too much of it.

Now consider how this affects the status of the sexes. Hume writes of this in his chapter on justice: 'Were there a species of creatures intermingled with men, which, though rational, were possessed of such inferior strength, both of body and mind, that they were incapable of all resistance, and could never, upon the highest provocation, make us feel the effects of their resentment; the necessary consequence, I think, is that we should be bound by the laws of humanity to give gentle usage to these creatures, but should not, properly speaking, lie under any restraint of justice with regard to them, nor could they possess any rights or property, exclusive of such arbitrary lords. Our intercourse with them could not be called society, which supposes a degree of equality; but absolute command on the one side, and servile obedience on the other ... This is plainly the situation of men, with regard to animals ... The great superiority of civilized Europeans above barbarous Indians, tempted us to imagine ourselves on the same footing with regard to them, and made us throw off all restraints of justice, and even of humanity, in our treatment of them. In many nations, the female sex are reduced to like slavery, and are rendered incapable of all property, in opposition to their lordly masters. But though the males, when united, have in all countries bodily force sufficient to maintain this severe tyranny, yet such are the insinuation, address, and charms of their fair companions, that women are commonly able to break the confederacy, and share with the other sex in all the rights and privileges of society.'[15]

The distinctions in power which are sustained by distinctions in economic power among men are here reflected in moral and political inequalities. Hume is right to identify relative strength, bodily, mental, and political, as a crucial issue. He observes that in some societies women are treated as powerless and exploited as slaves. It is to his credit that he opposes such doctrines and societies. His goal is apparently admirable: that women share with men all the rights and privileges of society. But questions remain. Does he envisage women having an *equal* share in these privileges? Apparently not, and there is further evidence to support this interpretation. First, there is another question requiring consideration.

Given that in a brute physical sense 'males, when united, have in all countries bodily force sufficient to maintain this severe tyranny,' what can women bring to bear in support of their claims? Hume has already distinguished mental power from physical, but does he argue that women have such intelligence or wisdom that they could make men feel the effects of their resentment? He does not. Have they moral or political strength – courage, or self-government – that they can command males in their turn? No. They have 'insinuation, address and charms.' These are 'qualities immediately agreeable to others,' and go some way toward crediting women with a source of social influence, but they are not the qualities attributed to his Cleanthes under this heading: wit with good manners, unaffected gallantry, and ingenious knowledge genteelly delivered. Insinuation, address, and charms are qualities thought more appropriate to women than to men. Moreover, the other three categories of virtue are entirely omitted. The woman is not presented as an equal counterpart to Cleanthes, but as a weak approximation to the male. She has qualities and virtues special to herself and inferior to the male's, but sufficient to earn her a place *of sorts* in civil society ('a *degree* of equality').

It is sometimes thought that the male-dominated property rights, which for writers like Locke and Hume are what constitute justice, are the only aberration an egalitarian need combat. If a woman were not 'incapable of all property' but could earn and own as well as a man, then her subordination would disappear from these accounts of civil society. Property laws, however, are only one aspect of the story. Physical, moral, and mental inequalities are also assumed by Hume, making his account thoroughly sexist.

Further evidence that this is in fact the view of women which Hume holds is found in the way he accounts for the pride which we feel in belonging to a good family with honourable forefathers of traceable antiquity, and preferably 'the uninterrupted proprietors of the same portion of land.' He adds: 'I have observ'd, that 'tis an additional subject of vanity, when they can boast, that these possessions have been transmitted thro' a descent compos'd entirely of males, and that the honours and fortune have never past thro' any female.' Hume endeavours to explain these phenomena: ''Tis a quality of human nature ... that the imagination naturally turns to whatever is important and considerable: and where two objects are presented to it, a small and a great one, usually leaves the former, and dwells entirely upon the latter. As in the society of marriage, the male sex has the advantage above the female, the husband first engages our attention; and ... [our] thought both rests upon him with greater satisfaction, and arrives at him with greater facility than his consort. 'Tis easy to see, that this property must strengthen the child's relation to the father, and weaken that to the mother ... This is the reason why children commonly bear their father's name, and are esteem'd to be of nobler or baser birth, according to *his* family. And tho' the mother shou'd be possest of a superior spirit and genius to the father, as often happens, the *general rule* prevails.'[16]

These discriminatory conclusions rest not only on the epistemological principle, that the imagination is drawn to the greater sooner than to the lesser, but also on the factual presupposition of inequality. My co-author will argue that these two (epistemological principle and factual observation) are so intimately connected in Hume that questions about their relative importance are not systematically determinable. At the present stage of the argument, we must conclude that Hume considers the human female distinctly inferior to the male, weaker both in mind and body, and graced by virtues which, although they gain her a lesser share in the rights and privileges of human society, are qualities peculiar to her and ones which are unsuitable and inadequate when found in males! 'An effeminate behaviour in a man, a rough manner in a woman; these are ugly because unsuitable to each character.'[17]

II *Hume's method in moral reasoning*

LOUISE MARCIL-LACOSTE

Hume's sexism, once recognized, may be seen in different ways, but there are serious objections against viewing his account of facts related to women as an ad hoc theme without philosophical significance. On a general basis, it would surely be odd to disregard the examples given by a philosopher whose moral reasoning is said to be based on a comparison of instances. In the case of women, this general argument becomes more specific when we consider the following features of Hume's account.

Hume's references to the situation of women are too numerous for them to be merely casual examples. Indeed, in the Treatise and the Enquiries alone, there are more than one hundred such references. The discussions of the woman question and the problem of chastity are too important in Hume's own view to be seen as a marginal theme in his moral reasoning. Indeed, the explanation of the different standards concerning the virtue of chastity for men and women is given by Hume as a proof that his general principles in morals are adequate. Hume's account of the situation of women is too consistently derived from his general principles to be seen as a piece of reasoning exhibiting the presence of an accidental double standard: the 'Humean' female is so far from being a misapplication of Hume's general principles that one must rather see it as an example of the consistency of his moral reasoning.[18]

Considering these features of Hume's account of women, one must thus admit that Hume's method in moral reasoning commits him to his sexist conclusions. This consideration, however, leads to another conclusion. Hume's moral philosophy and its method and principles seem to work as a philosophical justification of sexist discrimination.[19] Indeed, in taking Hume the moralist seriously one seems to be saying that the inferior status of women is quite consistent with utilitarian principles, and on this account, just. To put the matter differently: one may raise the question whether it is possible to accept Hume's reasoning and *not* participate in a philosophical justification of sexist discrimination.

It will be argued here that the answer to this question must be negative. There is no way of distinguishing between societal differences and social discrimination in Hume's method; there is no way to distinguish an 'is' from an 'ought' in the Humean account of such differences; and there is no methodological way of distinguishing between an explanation and a justification in Hume's general moral conclusions. In Hume's method of moral reasoning, these very ambiguities are present as facts, as puzzles or as answers, but not as moral problems; a point which suggests that sexist discrimination can hardly arise as a significantly moral and specific issue in the Humean framework.

In considering Hume's general method in morals from the point of view of a concern to avoid sexist discrimination, we first have to admit that 'discrimination' is a very ambiguous word. To discriminate is to distinguish two objects, two concepts, two facts, etc., *with precision*, a process which implies the recognition that one thing is different from another. In another sense, to discriminate is to separate things, concepts, facts, etc., *otherwise related*, or to analyse a complex network of factors by means of methodological categories of relations. In yet another sense, the sense we shall call derogatory, to discriminate is to distinguish one group from another to the *detriment* of one, or to distinguish one group from another in not treating one as well as the other.

Clearly, in discussing facts related to women, Hume does discriminate in *the first sense*. Not only does he recognize differences between men and women in questions related to chastity, pride, property, and politics, but he is able to detect the features of such differences with precision. His treatment of the virtue of chastity is a clear example of this. Hume identifies the difference between men and women as a difference in the degree of praise or blame attached to the observance or transgression of the virtue of chastity, this degree being higher in the case of women.[20]

In discussing facts related to women, Hume also discriminates in *the second sense*. When considering societal differences between the two sexes, he makes it clear that he wants to separate otherwise related factors, facts, opinions, etc., concerning people. His treatment of the political role of women is a good example of this. Admitting that in many

nations the female sex is reduced to slavery, Hume holds that notwithstanding the males' superior bodily force, women are 'commonly able to
break the confederacy and share with the other sex in all the rights and
privileges of society.' In politics, men and women are different with
respect to their relative share of natural and artificial virtues, but they
are for Hume otherwise related by means of the 'oblique' way in which
artificial virtues are related to natural ones.[21]

The third (derogatory) sense in which one may discriminate is also present in Hume's discussion of facts related to women; more precisely, his
descriptions are descriptions of discriminations taken in this sense. The
case of chastity is again a clear example. The difference between men and
women concerning this virtue is detrimental to women's share of 'pleasure to which nature has inspired so strong a propensity.' It is also detrimental to women's share of the 'accommodations' by which common
principles are usually applied according to circumstances, specifically in
being applied to women regardless of the age of parentage. It is a case of
not treating one group as well as another: the greater burden of restraint
to natural passions is imposed on women, while the interests served by
such a restraint are greater for men, whose parental (anatomical) insecurity is at stake here.[22]

Another example of discrimination in the third (derogatory) sense is
Hume's account of the issue of the transmission of honours and fortune
through a succession of males. The 'little to great' transition of the imagination explains that 'children commonly bear their father's name ... tho'
the mother should possest a superior spirit and genius to the father as
often happens.' Indeed, even when a 'superiority of this kind is so great'
as to be obvious, 'the general rule weakens the relation and makes a
break in the line of ancestors.' Here the distinction between men and
women is detrimental to women's share of the great side of the 'little to
great' transition of the imagination. It is also detrimental to women's
share of the 'medium betwixt a rigid stability and changeable and uncertain adjustment' which in principle the rules of justice seek. Women are
not treated as well as men: no matter how often and obviously counter-
instances could be found, the association of ideas between women and
little and men and great prevails. It should apparently prevail for otherwise the imagination would be 'at a loss' in ascribing property which, in
Hume's view, must be the full property of somebody.[23]

Discrimination in the third (derogatory) sense is also manifest in
Hume's account of the political role of women. For him, the suggestion
that women could be the masters and sovereigns is contrary to the com-

mon sentiments of mankind; the suggestion of a 'very free commerce between the sexes' in politics is contrary to the 'proper medium between the agreeable and the useful qualities of the sex,' while a proper regard to sex is a virtue. On a more general basis, Hume holds that the 'specious,' 'impracticable,' and 'extremely pernicious' idea of 'perfect equality' is contrary to history and to common sense. Here the distinction between men and women is detrimental to women's share of artificial virtues, by their relative confinement to private and to natural means and advantages. It is also detrimental to women's share of those standards by which one judges of fashion, vogue, custom, and law: those standards are specifically defined by 'departing from one's private situation,' while women are 'especially apt to overlook the remote motives.' Women are not treated as well as men: the standards of justice which must be traced 'a little higher' than in the variety of customs are to be found in those essential ideas of merit 'which prevail chiefly with regard to young men who can aspire to the agreeable qualities and may attempt to please.'

That Hume saw that the rules of justice function in a detrimental way for women is clear from his own statements of facts. The clearest example here is the case of pride related to titles and fortunes, because it strictly corresponds to Hume's own definition of prejudice, or a general rule we form rashly and which we maintain in spite of visible counter-instances. Hume's awareness of the detrimental aspect of the rules of justice for women may also be detected in his attempt to ascertain accurately the philosophical categories under which the instances he considers should be ranked.[24] Thus, the stricter rule of chastity for women is treated as an *exception* to the fact that rules of justice have no degree, an exception which is shown to be a 'still more conspicuous instance' of Hume's utilitarian principles, by means of the close-remote criterion. The exclusion of women from pride related to titles and fortune is treated as a plain *illustration* of the way in which the 'little to great' rule of the imagination is applied to questions of indivisible property and titles, notwithstanding the more specific rules of property. Finally, the limited political role of women is treated as a *consequence* of the scheme of balance between the natural and the artificial virtues by means of the relations between family and society as a whole, rather than as a result of the 'general scheme' of justice.[25]

The most significant fact about these illustrations of the senses in which Hume may be said to discriminate between men and women is that for someone concerned with sexist discrimination, Hume's framework provides no methodological way of distinguishing and assessing critically these three different meanings of discrimination. Indeed, as far as Hume's references to women are concerned, these three meanings are to be found in the same passages, and each would lead to equally valid interpretations from the point of view of his method in moral reasoning.

Clearly, one can read Hume's sexism from the point of view of his commitment to provide 'nice distinctions' and to distinguish in the attempt to find relations.[26] One can also read Hume's account of detriments suffered by women along the lines of his commitment to identify such 'original differences' as might be detectable from facts (such as the anatomical difference) and then show that such differences are the cause of all others and of their different influence upon our passions.[27] However, this simultaneity of meanings of discrimination makes it impossible to settle the specific moral issue of sexist discrimination in the derogatory sense within Hume's framework.[28]

It is significant for our purposes that in the case of chastity, the extension of the rules of justice above 'what merely arises from injustice' is given as the proof of a general fact about justice itself, not as a problem about it. It is also significant that the habitual exclusion of women from pride related to titles and fortune cannot appear as a 'mistake of right,' itself a species of immorality. The reason for this is that the general rule of the imagination is related to specific rules of property by virtue of Hume's method of distinguishing 'what particular goods are to be assigned to each particular person, while the rest of mankind are excluded from their possession and enjoyment.' Also significant is the fact that the definition of women's political role as a break in rather than a share of men's confederacy cannot be presented as 'blameable' in the context of the Humean connexions between natural and artificial virtues or in the context of Hume's view of the relations between family and society.

Though one can take Hume's sexism from several viewpoints which would be consistent with his method, one cannot correct Hume's sexist conclusions at will, knowing for example that there could be different and erroneous conclusions derived from the general principles of morality. Supposing one sees the inferior status of women as a prejudice in Hume's sense, then one is committed to correct such a prejudice by reflecting 'on the nature of superfluous and essential circumstances.' The standard of such reflection is to be found in the 'general tastes of mankind' which alone provide the specifications of the general utilitarian principles, pleasure and utility, for oneself and for others.[29] In order to correct Hume's sexist conclusions, one would thus have to appeal to those very principles which Hume has shown to be consistently applied in the case of women. In other words, Hume's methodological commitment to depict human nature as it is, never extending beyond experience, makes it impossible to raise experimentally the issue of sexist discrimination (in the derogatory sense) as the moral issue.[30] At best, it can be described as one of the features of 'facts' related to women.

A similar ambiguity awaits one who would wish to argue that however ambiguous the result of Hume's commitment to depict human nature could appear to someone concerned with avoiding sexist discrimination, it is wrong to interpret his conclusions on women as if he were presenting 'oughts' and 'ought nots.' Yet, to show that the inferior status of women is consistent with utilitarian principles is surely to do more than to list the opinions of mankind concerning women. In the Humean context, to show that the inferior status of women is consistently derived from the principles of pleasure and utility, for oneself and for others, is surely to propose as valid a judgment on the issue that would qualify *as moral*.

Clearly, Hume is aware that on account of their differences, the transition from 'is' to 'ought' expresses a new relation whose reason cannot lie in the fact that the latter would be deduced from the former. On the other hand, the very 'imperceptibility' of this transition is a problem concerning which one would need more than to observe that 'the distinction of vice and virtue is not founded merely on the relations of objects, nor is perceived by reason.'[31] The issue raised by the inferior status of women as a consistent application of utilitarian principles is that a sexist action which is said to be 'laudable' or 'blameable' – 'laudable' to Hume – cannot be critically challenged either as an 'is' or as an 'ought,' while Hume's very language on the status of women is characterized by what may be termed the conflation of 'ought' and 'is.'[32]

Consider, for example, Hume's statements that we *must* attach a greater degree than even required by justice to the blame or praise of the transgression or observance of chastity in the case of women. Hume puts this statement in the mouth of a philosopher who would examine the matter a priori. His own comment is that such a philosopher would be inclined to regard his conclusion as 'mere chimerical speculations' and his principles as 'more to be wished than hoped for in the world.' The superiority of the experimental philosopher here consists in the fact that a 'perfect knowledge of human nature' would convince him that objections to this a priori reasoning are 'easily got over in practice.' Hume concludes: according to the interest of civil society, the moral obligation concerning chastity must be proportioned according to sex. How is one to interpret Hume's 'must'? Surely, one must see it as a conditional 'ought' saying something like: given the common sentiments of mankind and the interest of civil society, it is necessary that women's infidelity should be more blameable than men's infidelity. Yet, as we know that in Hume's moral method we *must choose* the common view, or the common sentiments of mankind, and that we *ought never* to extend beyond experience, how is this conditional 'ought' to be taken?

Another example of a similar difficulty may be found in the ways in which Hume applies his complex notion of the natural and the artificial to customs related to women. One need not deny that custom is 'the sole guide to life,' nor commit the fallacy of identifying the natural with the virtuous or the unnatural with the vicious in order to see that, within Hume's framework, there is no way to raise as a moral issue the fact that women usually stand on the natural side of the natural/artificial scheme of balance. Not that Hume would generally offer unqualified statements on 'nature' or 'customs' when accounting for facts related to women, but precisely because his more qualified statements on such notions as related to women offer a paradigmatic case of his claim that the natural and the artificial are 'indistinguishable.'[33] Accordingly, the view that in the case of women the natural side *should* predominate in the 'proper equilibrium' between natural and artificial virtues is not a view that could be challenged either as an 'is' or as an 'ought,' while their conflation would seem unavoidable in the light of their consistency with utilitarian principles.

The argument here is not that Hume fails to see the difference between 'is' and 'ought' or that he fails to see the problem of deducing an 'ought' from an 'is.' The argument is rather that in treating 'ought' *as* 'is,' itself to be analysed according to a methodological 'ought' (such as 'we ought never to extend beyond experience') consistent with utilitarian principles, Hume makes it impossible to separate 'ought' and 'is' in his sexist account of facts related to women and that his method offers no way to settle this issue. On the contrary, merely because the stricter rule of chastity is a fact, it ought to be given as a moral rule, by virtue of the reality condition involved in the request never to extend beyond experience in moral reasoning. Besides, because this rule is derived from the 'infallible' sentiments of mankind, it also ought to be given as a 'just' moral rule, by virtue of the adequacy condition implied in the attempt to show that the utilitarian hypothesis is 'real and satisfactory.' Finally, because the only valid specifications of the general utilitarian hypothesis are those detected in the general tastes of mankind, the stricter rule of chastity for women ought to be given as the sole valid general rule, by virtue of the simplicity condition implied in the twofold attempt to stick to 'the most obvious case' and to avoid 'vulgar disputes' or disputes on degrees of virtues 'where the phenomena which can be produced in either side are so dispersed and uncertain and subject to so many interpretations that it is scarcely possible accurately to compare them or draw from them any determinate inference or conclusion.'

In considering these problems, one realizes that to claim here that for Hume 'whatever is may not be' or that for him 'we cannot derive an ought from an is' would be to blur the issue. Hume's framework apparently reduces all *invalid* oughts in moral reasoning to four classes: those derived from a priori reasoning upon immutable notions of intrinsic virtue, those rather to be wished than hoped for in human nature, those inconsistent with the common sentiments of mankind, and those inconsistent with utilitarian principles. It thus provides no means to assess critically some kinds of 'ought-nots' which are crucial in the attempt to avoid sexist discrimination: for example the possibility of saying that some 'is' (e.g. the detriments suffered by women) ought not to be, or that some 'ought' (e.g. women should be treated as inferior) ought not to be. In Hume's framework, one may notice with a sceptical smile that in the case of women, custom, which conceals itself best when it is the strongest, evidences a paradigmatic case of this 'kind of pre-established harmony between the course of nature and the succession of our ideas.'[34] In the case of practical philosophy one should add that it is because the rules of justice are not arbitrary that it would not be improper to call them laws of nature.[35]

As with the three meanings of discrimination, there is an ambiguity in the notion of explanation which it is important to remove in order to avoid sexist discrimination. For the sake of brevity, we can say that it should be possible to distinguish between a philosophical explanation of the inferior status of women and a philosophical justification of this inferior status as being morally just. In Hume's general account of the situation of women, however, it seems impossible to separate these two approaches, as the problems raised above on difference v. discrimination or is v. ought should already imply.

In point of fact, Hume makes it a methodological principle not to separate an explanation and a justification in as much as he insists on being a 'consistent anatomist,' rather than a 'painter of laudable traits.'

The anatomist's perspective is not one which Hume would describe as implying 'neutrality' or indifference to the issues. On the contrary, it is because we know that reason is perfectly inert or that reason can at most be a mediate cause of action that we know that moral philosophy is quite different from speculative philosophy. As Hume puts it, 'because the subject is not indifferent to us, our reasoning should appear more real and solid.'[36] The anatomist is indeed useful by proposing accurate and just reasoning, even when he presents 'to the eye the most hideous and disagreeable objects.'

Here, however, Hume's account of facts related to women can hardly be labelled as an account of something which either is 'hideous' or 'disagreeable' to the general tastes of mankind. This suggests that in order to raise the issue of sexism, we cannot rely on Hume's refusal to be a painter of laudable traits. It would seem that we have to test whether Hume's account of the justice of women's inferior status really is the expression of the 'natural unprejudiced reason,' avoiding systems and hypotheses that have perverted it.

But here again, it would seem that one is deprived of methodological means because of Hume's rather limited view of what can count as a 'sufficient explanation.' As he puts it, 'in all enquiries concerning these moral distinctions, it will be sufficient to shew the principles which make us feel a satisfaction or uneasiness from the survey of any character, in order to satisfy us why the character is laudable or blameable ... In giving a reason therefore for the pleasure and uneasiness we sufficiently explain the vice or virtue ... we need not go farther into the cause of our satisfaction.'[37] Clearly, in saying that one need not go farther into the cause of our satisfaction, Hume is objecting to those moral reasoners who would like to appeal to what is 'utterly inaccessible to the understanding.' Yet, one need not appeal to 'obscure origins' of moral approval to see that Hume's notion of a 'sufficient explanation' makes it impossible to distinguish between an explanation and a justification of sexist discrimination; especially if we add to the sufficient causes of mankind's (apparent) satisfaction, the demonstration that such causes are consistent with the utilitarian hypothesis.

For example, one may ask why the reference to the general rules of the imagination should sufficiently explain the inferiority of women in matters related to title and fortune, given the fact it would seem to contradict Hume's warning that 'if we look for a solution in the imagination it is impossible to give them [qualities] any precise bound or termination.' However, at this point, Hume is not unphilosophically running 'from one principle to its contrary according to particular phenomenon.'[38] His explanation of this fact is 'sufficient,' because in Hume's general model of a distinction between a belief and mere fictions of the imagination the distinguishing principle is custom. In the case of customs related to pride, the general rules of the imagination are specified by virtue of the utilitarian hypothesis according to which it is useful to society that property should belong to somebody, in our case, to the 'most considerable part,' the males. This explanation is sufficient: it not only remains within the realm of experience, it also shows the observable cause of pride and, further, shows how such causes are consistent with utilitarian principles.

Of course, Hume holds that general rules may change, if circumstances render necessary a revision of the general scheme in such a way that the latter is evidently susceptible of serious improvement; but given his account of facts related to women, what could count as an evidently serious improvement? In what sense could one take the status of women as presented by Hume to be a result of superstition? Further, how could sexist political discrimination arise as a significant issue, given that Hume holds that by mere virtue of time conventions become natural and we imagine, for example, some people born to submit and others with the right to command – 'the right to authority' being 'nothing but the constant possession of it.'[39]

It would thus seem that in reducing the notion of a sufficient explanation in morals to the showing of experimentally detectable causes of pleasure or uneasiness whose compatibility with utilitarian principles may be indicated, Hume makes it impossible to distinguish an experimental explanation of the inferior status of women from a philosophical justification of this inferiority as being morally just. Clearly, one can take his general conclusions both ways, either insisting on the epistemological limits of Hume's experimental model for moral reasoning or insisting on the utilitarian consistency of his account of sexist discrimination.

To the above arguments, one might object that there are many principles in Hume's moral method and epistemology which could be fruitfully used as a basis to advocate changes in sexist conventions. A would-be feminist might welcome Hume's insistence on custom, his willingness to describe unpleasant facts, his realistic reminders that we can change circumstances rather than (directly) change human sentiments, and even Hume's account of the role of the imagination in morals. One may indeed hope to use such statements, especially Hume's sceptical statements, as a basis for advocating changes in sexist conventions: what is called 'natural' may be shown to be conventional; what is presented as 'equality' may be seen as factually detrimental to women; what is presented as 'reasonable' may be shown to be based on the 'slightest' analogy, and even what is said to be consistent with utilitarian principles may be shown to be much less agreeable and useful than a proposed alternative.[40]

What is striking in such attempts, however, is the fact that those principles which could be used in order to advocate changes in sexist conventions are all general principles taken outside of Hume's specified ways of reasoning upon them, especially in morals. Furthermore, we know that for Hume we should 'cut off all loose discourses' and reduce them to 'something that is precise and and exact.' Hume insists that the establishment of general rules is purposeless while remaining in general terms, and despises any system the terms of which are not explained. As a matter of fact, the most important of Hume's requests to his reader is that we should not alter his definitions.[41]

The conclusion is that we cannot take Hume's general principles at will, without introducing the way in which he specifies their meanings and relations. But if we do that, we have to recognize the consistency of his account of facts related to women. We also have to admit that this consistency is the reason the ambiguities of his sexism cannot be removed by means of Hume's *own* specified framework. In other words, in order to use Hume's moral methodology in the attempt to avoid sexist discrimination, one would have to refer to Hume's principles in a specified manner which is not Humean.

Thus, to the question whether one can take Hume, the moralist, seriously and not participate in a philosophical justification of sexist discrimination, the final answer must be negative. As in Hume's framework there is no methodological way of removing the ambiguities in his sexist account of facts related to women, and as his account is a consistent utilitarian account of sexist discrimination,[42] there is no way to make sure that in following Hume one does *not* justify sexism philosophically, while there are quite a few ways in which one could show that this is exactly what we do. In as much as these ambiguities of sexism must be removed in any philosophical system refusing to offer a justification of sexism, it is better not to rely on Hume. As it turns out, Hume's sexism is surely not a case of vulgar sexism. It is rather one of the most sophisticated and subtle examples of still popular forms of 'intellectual' sexism. It is high time to suggest that vulgar sexism is NOT the worst kind.

Some of the research for part II of this paper was supported by the Ministère de l'Education, FCAC, Québec. I am grateful to David F. Norton for his comments on this essay.

NOTES AND REFERENCES

This two-part essay is a development of a previous collaboration. See Steven Burns 'The Humean Female' and Louise Marcil-Lacoste 'The Consistency of Hume's Position Concerning Women' *Dialogue* xv (1976) 415–24 and 425–40. Major portions of the former have been reused with permission.

1 See, for example, Mary Shaw Kuypers' defence of this view in her *Studies in the Eighteenth Century Background of Hume's Empiricism* (New York 1966) especially chapters 5 and 6.
2 It would not be consistent with this interpretation to find in his distinction between 'is' and 'ought' reason for thinking that Hume held what is now called 'naturalism' to be a fallacy. His main target is rationalism.
3 *Enquiries concerning Human Understanding and concerning the Principles of Morals* ed L.A. Selby-Bigge (Oxford 1894) 173-4
4 This woman was Hippolyte de Saujeon, comtesse de Boufflers, the celebrated 'Madam Blewflower.' See, for instance, J.Y.T. Greig *David Hume* (New York 1931) chapters 19 and 22.
5 *Enquiries* 270
6 Ibid
7 *A Treatise of Human Nature* ed L.A. Selby-Bigge (Oxford 1888) 570-1; compare 'An infidelity ... is much more pernicious in *women* than in men' (*Enquiries* 207).
8 *Enquiries* 238–9
9 Ibid 239
10 Ibid 206–7
11 *Treatise* 570–1; see also 479–80 and 518, where Hume explains that natural parental affection is a duty. Natural sentiment is the basis of this affection, with duty invoked only when sentiment momentarily fails.
12 Ibid 572
13 Charles W. Hendel ed *David Hume's Political Essays* (New York 1953) lvii
14 *Enquiries* 194
15 Ibid 190–1
16 Ibid 308–9

17 Ibid 266. In 'A Dialogue,' his spokesman describes a nation which 'gravely exalts those, whom nature has subjected to [men], and whose inferiority and infirmities are absolutely incurable. The women, though without virtue, are their masters and sovereigns' (*Enquiries* 332). Now this is parody. Palamedes, his interlocutor, has just caricatured ancient Athens (disguised as 'Fourli'). The other's rejoinder, as Palamedes quickly recognizes, is a parody of contemporary France. Even allowing, however, for exaggeration appropriate to the context, this passage makes clear Hume's conviction that there are 'absolutely incurable' natural limits to the extent to which women can participate in, let alone usurp, the political roles of men.

18 For a more detailed analysis see Marcil-Lacoste 'Consistency'; the present analysis is an attempt to answer the questions raised in the conclusion of that article.

19 Hume's treatments of different classes and races should also be compared along with the extent to which his method is determined by historical and material circumstances. I merely hope to show in this paper that any 'neutralist' account of Hume's method would be inadequate.

20 *Treatise* 571; *Enquiries* 231

21 *Treatise* 197, 483–4, 530; *Enquiries* 191–7. Hume holds that natural virtues are shared by men and women, equally so in private areas such as the family ('Consistency' 427–9).

22 *Treatise* 533, 571; *Enquiries* 207–8

23 *Treatise* 308, 511–14. Hume's account of 'facts' relating to women owes much to his model for property and economics.

24 'Every quality and action of every human being must by this means [sentiments arising from humanity] be ranked under some class or denomination expressive of general censure or applause' (*Enquiries* 273).

25 See Hume's objections to the patriarchal theory of the origin of government in *Treatise* 499, 541; *Enquiries* 190ff.

26 This is the point of Hume's experiments (see *Treatise* 332–47) and of his Baconian *experimentum crucis* (*Enquiries* 219).

27 *Treatise* 300

28 In his speculative philosophy, Hume has argued that the notion of difference is the negation of a relation rather than a relation itself (i.e. something real and positive in itself); see *Treatise* 15, 18, and cf ibid 464.

29 Ibid 148–9; *Enquiries* 165, 268–9, 336

30 *Treatise* 466; *Enquiries* 273

31 *Treatise* 404–70

32 In morals, facts include passions, motives, volitions, thoughts, tempers, situations, and so on (ibid 404–5). In reasoning upon them, we regard a new fact, the general tastes of mankind (*Enquiries* 135).

33 *Treatise* 530, cf ibid 573.
34 *Enquiries* 55
35 *Treatise* 484
36 *Enquiries* 9–16
37 *Treatise* 471
38 The philosopher knows that 'its seeming uncertain in some instances proceeds from the secret opposition of contrary causes' and that therefore 'the irregular events, which outwardly discover themselves, can be no proof that the laws of nature are not observed with the greatest regularity in its internal operations and government' (*Enquiries* 87).
39 *Treatise* 554–63, 566
40 Custom may render something more valuable than another, while the other would in fact be more valuable. Hume's moral argument against counter-factual proposals (such as the Levellers' utopia) is that they would require tyranny in order to be carried out (ibid 495–6, 503).
41 Ibid 407
42 There are, of course, important differences in method among Hume, Bentham, and John Stuart Mill, despite the utilitarian cast of their approach. I am concerned here with an examination of Hume's method rather than with utilitarian thought in general.

Hegel and 'The Woman Question': Recognition and intersubjectivity

PATRICIA JAGENTOWICZ MILLS

Hegel wrote: 'When the power of unity disappears from men's lives ... then the need for philosophy arises.' He was talking literally about men since he did not believe women capable of philosophical understanding. Nevertheless, if we broaden Hegel's own narrow angle of vision to include women, we can see that woman's need for philosophy comes from just such a lack of unity: the fragmentation which comes from the separation of work and home life. The realization of the oppressive and joyless roles assigned to us led us to attempt a refusal: we would not have our lives pre-packaged and sold behind our backs. But the moment of our awakening has passed and the immediacy and unity of the woman's movement is no longer here to sustain us. We are therefore forced into remembering and understanding.[1]

For woman, the task is to understand her oppression in relation to the development of capitalism and bourgeois society. We must search for the liberating potential as well as understanding the negative aspects of that development. In our search, philosophy offers a way to comprehend where we have been, where we are, and where we might go together: it offers the conceptual and analytic understanding through which we may develop theory, practice, and strategy. But the philosophic tradition never talks *to* woman and only sometimes concedes to talk *about* her thereby reflecting and reinforcing her oppression.[2] By inserting the historical reality of woman's place into the philosophic tradition we make the tradition more self-reflective: through such self-reflection the male domination which either obliterates woman or makes her a 'sentence in a system' may be exorcised so that philosophy may become a truly *human* project.

We must begin with an analysis of the family because it is here that woman's oppression begins. We must examine how work, property, sexuality, love, and ego-development in a patriarchal-capitalist society are to be understood in terms of the family as we examine the relation between the working class and the bourgeois family. But an analysis of 'the family' often obscures the *woman* question. If, as Marx says, the turning of the subject into the predicate requires a revolutionary turn through the application of the transformative method, then for any 'revolution' to have meaning for woman she must emerge as the subject, making the family the predicate of her existence. And, while Marx's theoretical understanding of the dialectic of capitalism grounded in material and historical processes is accepted here as fundamentally correct, since woman does not describe a class or a caste but a *sex*, the project of integrating her specific oppression into a Marxist analysis is complex. While neither the family nor woman's oppression can be understood apart from an analysis of capitalism in its present form, the categories of political economy are the categories of 'civil society' and cannot simply or strictly be applied to the sphere of the family because of the specific and unique social relations within the family. Thus, while we must analyse the development of capitalism (from its private to its corporate structure) and we must analyse the relationship of the family to civil society in terms of the class content of the family, we must also recognize that as a specific sphere of everyday life, the family has its own specific logic and does not simply mirror the relations of production.

Marx owes much to Hegel but in his move away from Hegel's tripartite structure of family, civil society, and state, to concentrate on political economy as the science of civil society, Marx cannot grasp the specific nature of woman's oppression which stems from her position in the family. The specificity of the three spheres must be maintained even as we understand their dynamic interrelationship. And Hegel's philosophical system must be understood if we are to ground the tasks outlined above because his dialectical analysis not only acknowledges the specificity of the sphere of the family but his account of intersubjectivity implies the equal recognition of woman even though Hegel himself is tied to a framework which prevents him from *actually* seeing woman as man's equal.

For the purposes of this paper we shall be limited to a schematic outline of the Hegelian project within the framework of my emphasis on 'the woman question.' We shall ultimately focus on Hegel's analysis of the dialectic of recognition and the need for the Other. While the master-slave relation in the *Phenomenology*, as well as some aspects of Hegel's *Logic* and his *Philosophy of Nature*, must be considered, it is in the *Philosophy of Right* that woman's connection to Hegel's concept of 'first nature' represents the philosophical culmination of the theme of the family as a 'preserve' within which woman is kept like a dangerous species while man moves into the spheres of political and economic activity to develop his 'second nature.'

Any brief attempt to recapitulate Hegel's philosophy is always inadequate and risks being 'abstract,' or partial, and therefore 'false.' Nevertheless, without a brief sketch of Hegel's system the significance of my emphasis on 'the woman question' would not be clear.

Hegel's *Phenomenology of Spirit*, published in 1807, is a philosophy of experience, an analysis of human consciousness from its most primitive beginnings to the highest stage of absolute knowledge. The analysis starts with an epistemological orientation that advances from sensation to perception and understanding, and culminates in self-conscious reason. In each progressive stage, consciousness seeks to know the object directly and immediately; the ways in which the object appears to consciousness are at the same time the processes by which consciousness discovers the significance of the object. In a teleological movement consciousness becomes self-consciousness, self-consciousness becomes reason, reason becomes Spirit and Spirit becomes the universe's knowledge of itself.[3]

In each of these progressive stages the same dialectical logic of becoming is at work. Each stage, while in itself reasonable, is 'abstract' or partial, because it leaves out its essential opposite. Thus, as consciousness seeks to know the object immediately and directly, a contradictory 'moment' emerges. A profound struggle takes place between the two 'moments' from which emerges a 'moment' that simultaneously maintains, negates, and transcends the earlier 'moments.' This is a complex process for which Hegel uses a single term: the original 'moments' are *aufgehoben*.* Spirit, continually struggling with what appears to be something other than it, goes through a process of diremption or alienation, and finally 'returns to itself' when everything that has seemed to be other is completely appropriated or subjectivized. It is in the final 'concrete' understanding of the totality, where the opposites are reconciled, that the truth is to be found.[4]

---

* *Aufgehoben* is the past participle of the verb *aufgeheben*; *Aufhebung* is the noun. The German includes all three elements – preservation or maintenance, negation, and transcendence – of a process which may occur instantaneously or over time; there is no simple translation.

Hegel wishes to maintain an 'ontogenetic principle' such that the stages of Spirit's movement are repeated in the 'universal individual.' The development of Spirit is to be told in both objective and subjective terms; the historical stages of development that the human race goes through are recapitulated in the psychological development of the 'universal individual.'[5]

The analysis of the problem of the Other in the *Phenomenology* depicts human self-consciousness (being-for-itself) as rooted in desire. Self-consciousness is mediation and as such it reveals the relation between desire and the object of desire. In the initial stages of the development of self-consciousness the object of desire is organic or animal life envisioned as totality. Later, the desire for life appears as something alien, something external to and other than the self while simultaneously remaining identical with the self. As we become aware of our life as alien to us, we estrange or dirempt ourselves from it and thereby negate it. The life of the self becomes an object for the self and self-consciousness exists through an exchange with the world. But self-consciousness, as human existence, is possible only when it is recognized by another self-consciousness in the conflict between being-for-itself and being-for-other.

Thus the Hegelian self, as desire, needs the Other in such a way that the Other becomes an ontological condition for the existence of self. The desire that constitutes the self exists only if it is an object of another desire. Human desire becomes the desire for the desire of the Other. Since each self-consciousness must be recognized by another, recognition grounds the universality of self-consciousness. Our self-consciousness is mirrored in the Other such that it not only achieves a being-for-itself, but also sees itself as external and determined, as a being-for-others. And the same process takes place for the Other. By virtue of the Hegelian dialectic of mutual recognition, each self is conscious of itself as a self and inter-subjectivity is grounded. The reciprocity of the self's desire for recognition from an Other offers a philosophical perspective of human existence necessarily based on intersubjectivity.[6] (As we shall see, this necessity is not met in the relation between man and woman in marriage, as it is characterized by Hegel. I shall argue, therefore, that Hegel's system does not permit woman to be viewed as fully human.)

If primary desire is desire for organic life, then, according to Hegel, for us to become aware of ourselves as human, distinct from organic life, there must be opposition to the natural order. In human consciousness this opposition occurs through the risk of life. As each self-consciousness demands from the Other the recognition without which it could not exist, there occurs a life and death struggle. Each self-consciousness intends the death of the Other in this struggle for recognition because each one desires not only to be recognized as pure being-for-itself by the Other but wants to suppress its limited or determined representation as a being-for-the-Other.[7] Hegel describes this fundamental struggle of life: 'it is solely by risking life that freedom is obtained, only thus is it tried and proved that the essential nature of self-consciousness is not bare existence, is not the merely immediate form in which it at first makes its appearance, is not its mere absorption in the expanse of life. Rather it is thereby guaranteed that there is nothing present but what might be taken as a vanishing moment – that self-consciousness is merely pure self-existence, being-for-itself.'[8] To be a truly human being one must be willing to risk one's life and aim at the death of the Other in a struggle for recognition. Thus, this necessary intersubjectivity is a hostile one, a kind of Hobbesian 'each against each.'

When we look for the historical perspective of Hegel's ontological encounter we find it first in his section on 'Lordship and Bondage.' Here domination grounds not only intersubjectivity but also the process of objectification. If, in the life and death struggle for recognition, one self-consciousness literally succeeds in destroying the Other the project does not succeed because death becomes an 'abstract negation, not the negation characteristic of consciousness which cancels in such a way that it preserves and maintains what is sublated and thereby survives its being sublated [i.e. *aufgehoben*].' If, however, the struggle ends in such a way that both survive, then a relationship of negation is established which is one of dominance or subjugation. One self-consciousness is 'independent, and its essential nature is to be, for itself; the other is dependent, and its essence is life or existence for another. The former is the Master, or Lord, the latter the Bondsman.'

But in a dialectical turn Hegel points out that the master or lord *needs* a slave or bondsman and the objects he produces in such a way as to defeat the master's search for independence. In an attempt to become an independent self-consciousness, the lord or master has enslaved himself. 'The truth of the independent consciousness is accordingly the consciousness of the bondsman.' While the master's relation to the slave is mediated by the objects the slave produces and his relation to the objects is mediated by the slave, the essential nature of the slave is expressed in the things he produces. In the process of work as objectification, the slave's consciousness 'is bound up with an independent being or with thinghood in general.'[9] Through his work the slave masters nature and thereby achieves a freedom from nature and sense of self which the master lacks. This domination of nature through work transforms the 'natural' world to create history. Thus, the slave who prefers life to death and saves himself by surrendering his claim for recognition nevertheless creates an independent self through the process of labour as objectification. But Hegel's idea of freedom here is a purely interior reality which the slave experiences while remaining enslaved.

As we have outlined above, it is with the consciousness of death that a truly human existence begins. Hegel says of the slave that his 'consciousness was not in peril and fear for this element or that, nor for this or that moment of time, it was afraid for its entire being, it felt the fear of death, the sovereign master.'[10] This fear of death is the negativity which haunts our self-consciousness and transforms our limited or determined being into free being. The slave internalizes this negativity and transforms existence through the process of objectification so that the world is no longer a merely natural 'given.' The slave creates a human world and the negativity of his own self-consciousness achieves consistency and stability through work. Thus labour and the struggle to the death for unilateral recognition are the conditions of self-consciousness: they *ground* history as they make it possible.[11]

The master-slave dialectic reverberates in the writings of many philosophers and political theorists who see in it the quintessence of Hegel's thought. Marx picks up Hegel's category of objectification as it is first developed in this paradigm and shows the effects of objectification grounded in domination: work or labour which is rooted in the domination of others is a central point of his critique of capitalism. Marx praises Hegel for having understood that we develop through our own activity and he, like Hegel, challenges the ontological division between the person or subject and the thing that person creates. Although Marx alters Hegel's idea somewhat, for both Hegel and Marx the product or object is neither merely external nor indifferent to the nature of the person who has produced it. Simone de Beauvoir, in *The Second Sex*, claims that certain passages in the section on the master-slave dialectic are more germane to an analysis of the relationship between man and woman, for woman, if not man's slave, has always been dependent on him: woman has always suffered from male domination and is the most perfect example of the dependent consciousness. Mary O'Brien, in her dissertation on 'The Politics of Reproduction,' shows clearly and concisely how de Beauvoir's analysis of woman in *The Second Sex* as the dependent slave consciousness described by Hegel is incomplete and inadequate. According to de Beauvoir since woman has not participated in productive labour and has not made history all she can do is aspire to transcendence – a transcendence defined in terms of male values. But transcendence in her existentialist philosophy is not the acceptance of values second-hand but rather the affirmation and realization of a project. De Beauvoir never considers the implication for woman that within his dependence the slave recreates the world to create history. While the slave labours and creates, woman in de Beauvoir's view simply adopts the possibility of freedom she has been *shown* by man, and does not, like Hegel's slave, *create* that possibility. Freedom for woman is reduced in her analysis from being a confrontation with otherness to being an act of mimesis: woman does not confront man as the Other but merely mimics his attempt to realize his freedom. De Beauvoir misses the crucial point that woman neither is, nor can be, master or slave in Hegel's schema precisely because, for Hegel, woman does not experience a contradiction between herself and nature which she must negate.[12]

If we want to appropriate critically the master-slave dialectic to illuminate the relations between the sexes as well as to illuminate the relations between the classes, we must bear in mind that 'Lordship and Bondage' is only one brief moment in the Hegelian schema of the movement of Spirit toward universal self-knowledge. For Hegel it is neither work (as objectification) nor the dialectic of dependent-independent consciousness that is most significant; rather, it is self-consciousness finding itself in an Other equal self which is required for the reconciliation that leads to universal self-consciousness. The truth of self-consciousness is not the 'I' but the 'we,' the 'Ego that is "we"', a plurality of Egos, and "we" that is a single Ego.'[13] This process of mutual recognition, as I have mentioned, will be shown to necessarily exclude woman.

In Hegel's analysis of the process of recognition, and of the master-slave dialectic, there is no mention of woman (master and slave are both seen as males even though historically many slaves were women). When we go looking for woman in the *Phenomenology* we must proceed to the section on the pagan ethical world and, more specifically, to the family. In this section we learn that history can be understood as a dialectic of particular and universal: man seeks recognition of his own particular self from all men; he seeks universal recognition of his particularity. And universality, as the *Aufhebung* of the opposition between particular and universal, is 'concrete' or universal individuality. Thus Spirit moves from immediate, undifferentiated unity (bare abstract universality) through difference and particularization to the concrete unity of universal and particular.

However, in the pagan world, the dialectical opposition between the particular and the universal cannot be overcome and this opposition resolves itself in such a way that woman, who never achieves self-consciousness precisely because she never leaves the family, causes the demise of the pagan world.

Man is necessarily a member of a family and the family is the sphere of the particularity of the pagan male's existence. Within the family, man is *this* particular father, *this* husband, *this* son and not simply *a* father, *a* husband, *a* son. But the family is the sphere of 'merely natural existence,' 'mere particularity,' and as such its supreme value is essentially inactive biological existence or animal life. While man has particularity inside the family circle, it is an unconscious particularity because, within this circle, there is no negating action – no risk of life for recognition. Within the family man cannot achieve self-consciousness or truly human satisfaction because the truly human demands the conscious risk of life.[14]

While neither male nor female can achieve self-consciousness within the family, the male moves out to become a citizen: 'Because it is only as a citizen that he is real and substantial, the individual, when not a citizen, and belonging to the family, is merely unreal insubstantial shadow.'[15] The pagan state however, only recognizes or realizes the universal aspect of human action and risk while the particular remains embedded in the family. There is a fundamental antinomy between family life as the natural ground of ethical life and ethical life in its social universality in the state. Hegel writes that within the state 'the community is that substance in the form of self-consciously realized action' which is in opposition to the family as 'the other side' which 'has the form of immediate or directly existent substance.' The community draws man away from the family: by subduing his 'merely natural existence' and his 'mere particularity' the state induces him to live 'in and for the universal.' What is achieved in the state, through action and risk, is 'the manhood of the community.' But while the universal aspect of a man's existence is recognized by the state, this existence is not truly *his*: it is not *he* as a particular who is recognized by the state. By acting on behalf of the state man's action achieves universality at the expense of his particularity. The *Aufhebung* of the familial particular and the political universal which results in concrete or universal individuality is possible only in death in the pagan world.[16]

In the pagan world the transcendence of death in and by historical memory is achieved through the family. The ethical relation between the members of the family is not that of sentiment or love but duty in connection with burying and remembering the dead as well as avenging them if need be. Through these obligations to the dead the 'powerless bare particular unity of family life is raised to universal individuality.' Since familial life does not depend on the activity of the members but simply on their being, their inaction, death changes nothing in the value attributed to and by the family. And by burying and remembering the family members, the family maintains the continuity of the human community through time.

In life, the family and state, the particular and universal spheres of man's existence, are mutually exclusive. The family represents life and the state represents the risk of life. In the pagan world the conflict between these two spheres is inescapable and unalterable: man cannot renounce the family since he cannot renounce the particularity of his existence nor can he renounce the universality of his action in and for the state. Since the particular is not included in the universal sphere of the state, the state is not truly universal and the *Aufhebung* of particular and universal is not possible in the life of the pagan world. Thus pagan man is as little satisfied by his existence as a citizen as he is by his family life and the conflict between the familial and the political make for the tragic character of pagan life.[17] It should be noted that this entire discussion refers to the 'masters' of the pagan world but not to the 'slaves.'

For Hegel the conflict between state and family, universal and particular, is also a conflict between human and divine law as represented in the conflict between man and woman. 'Nature,' he writes, 'assigns woman to the divine law and man to human law.' Thus while the political life of the pagan state represents the 'manhood of the community,' the family is the sphere of womanhood.

When we attempt to isolate and focus on woman's role in Hegel's schema some critical discontinuities emerge which stem from the fact that she never leaves the family. While the son 'leaves the immediate, rudimentary and therefore negative ethical life of the family to produce the concrete ethical order which is conscious of itself,' the daughter merely moves into another family situation by marrying and becoming a wife. Hegel wants to claim that there is reciprocal recognition between husband and wife in the marriage, but this recognition is 'natural self-knowledge,' not ethical life.

A woman's *ethical* relation is not to feeling or the sentiment of love but, rather, is a relation to the universal. In an ethical household: 'a woman's relationships are not based on a reference to this particular husband, this particular child, but to *a* husband, to children *in general*, – not to feeling, but to the universal ... So far, then, as particularity is implicated in this relationship in the case of the wife, her ethical life is not purely ethical; so far, however, as it is ethical, the particularity is a matter of indifference, and the wife is without the moment of knowing herself as *this* particular self in and through an other.'[18] To the extent that particularity is implicated in the relationship between husband and wife, it is not ethical; yet, *in her case*, Hegel claims it makes no difference. The husband gains an unconscious particularity as *this* husband through the wife's exercise of universal recognition of him as *a* husband while never achieving particularity herself. He is particularized but she is not: man, says Hegel, gains particularity in the family precisely because he leaves this sphere to achieve universal recognition in the political sphere but woman never enters the political sphere; she is caught and bound within the immediacy of the family circle.

In keeping with his Christian heritage, Hegel is in search of the perfect *non-sexual* relationship between a man and a woman. He believes he has found his ideal in the brother-sister relation because 'brother and sister ... do not desire one another.' While Freud's theories and anthropological studies of incest taboos would seem to make such an assertion at least dubious if not altogether untenable, Hegel believes that this lack of desire offers woman, as sister, some form of equal recognition. Brother and sister are 'free individualities with respect to each other' in a way that surpasses the husband-wife relationship which is complicated by sexual desire. But again, this brother-sister relation is not one of *conscious* ethical life; rather, the law of the family is the sister's immediate, unconscious nature.

Hegel claims that woman's universal substance *and* her particularity are to be found by fulfilling her familial duties. And he wants to claim that there is equal or mutual recognition between husband and wife in the pagan world. Yet when we look closely we see that this mutual relation is not that of ethical life, and when it *is* ethical life there is no mutuality because the woman never achieves precisely what one is to gain from mutual recognition, i.e. particularity. In the familial ethical life between man and woman, man gains particularity through the wife's relation to the universal, even though the woman is never a particular self. While man can not renounce the particularity of his being, woman never achieves it. She cannot achieve an independent self-consciousness within the immediacy of the 'ethical' family and she is not allowed out into any other sphere of life. Since woman's 'recognition' always takes place *inside* the family she must remain the walking dead of 'unreal insubstantial shadow.' In the Hegelian schema woman cannot even achieve the self-consciousness of the slave because she does not *do* anything – she is not seen as being involved in the process of work as objectification or world creation. She has no universal recognition of her action or humanity in the state – she is not seen as someone who *acts* but merely as someone who *is* – and thus has no particularity in the family. Hegel's attempt to assert simply that woman finds both particularity and universality in the family contradicts his own analysis of how one can achieve particularity. And, in his schema, a woman without a brother never achieves even a glimmer of an unconscious self that might be the equal of man's.

The question of exactly how woman can represent the sphere of particularity while never knowing herself as a particular is a question never addressed by Hegel. 'Nature,' according to him, has assigned woman to the sphere of immediacy and he keeps her imprisoned there on nature's behalf: while man finds a self-conscious reality or second nature in the community, woman remains in the sphere of immediate biological life, the sphere of first nature. Hegel does not feel impelled to look behind or beyond first nature when he treats woman in the *Phenomenology*. The historical 'Ego' that is 'we,' which Hegel has attempted to ground in recognition and labour, is an all-male one.

The tragic conflict in pagan society between the universalistic state and the particularistic family ends in the destruction of the pagan world. Since particularity is not *included* in the state, it destroys the state. And, woman, as representative of the family principle, the principle of particularity which the state represses, is the direct cause of the downfall of the pagan world: 'Since the community gets itself subsistence only by breaking in upon family happiness, and dissolving (individual) self-consciousness into the universal, it creates its enemy for itself within its own gates, creates it in what it suppresses, and what is at the same time essential to it – womankind in general. Womankind – the everlasting irony in the life of the community – changes by intrigue the universal purpose of government into a private end, transforms its universal activity into a work of this or that specific individual, and perverts the universal property of the state into a possession and ornament for the family.'[19] Woman as representative of the immediacy of family life and the principle of particularity revolts and destroys the community in the pagan world by acting on the young man – she persuades him to exercise power for the family dynasty rather than for public welfare.[20]

While Hegel claims that woman acts on behalf of particularity, as I see it, she never achieves particularity – what prompts her to this intrigue is her confinement to the sphere of the family and the limitation to the immediate. Woman acts as the agent of destruction in the pagan world because she represents immediacy and as Hegel says, 'immediacy contains a contradiction: it is at once the unconscious peace of nature and the self-conscious unresting peace of spirit.'[21]

It is important to note a connection between Hegel's philosophy of nature and his conception of woman. Fackenheim describes how, for Hegel, philosophical thought can both recognize and conquer the actual world because, after having been brought forth by the Idea, nature gradually supersedes all natural determinations and passes over into Spirit as its higher truth. Nature itself, as contingent and immediate, is seen as Other than Spirit and as the necessary pre-condition for Spirit's self-knowledge: it is sleeping mind/spirit. But ultimately this 'first' nature is 'overreached' by Spirit in Spirit's movement towards universal self-knowledge. Thus Hegel's attempt to include dialectically all opposi-tional 'moments' presents us with an abstract negation: nature itself, as immediate and contingent, cannot be fully comprehended in the logical Idea. It cannot be raised in itself to an essence above contingency and the concept can never completely master experience. In an effort to preserve contingency in his system Hegel ultimately denies it.[22]

In a similar manner, we discover, in the *Philosophy of Right*, that woman seems to deserve some rights in the sphere of second nature for she, like man, is human. But woman does not enter the sphere of second nature on her own and ultimately she, like first nature, remains Other, tied to the immediate. In fact, her tie to the immediate is necessary for the Hegelian schema as Hegel tries to maintain or preserve first nature as well as to transcend it: man is to gain access to first nature through woman as woman is to gain access to second nature through man. But without passing through negativity via a contradiction between herself and first nature, and without *direct* access to the sphere of second nature, woman cannot be truly human in the Hegelian schema.

Unlike man, who gains a 'second nature' in his economic and political life, the limitation of woman's life in and to 'first nature' forces her to sacrifice her claim to self-consciousness. Woman, like nature, does not *act* in Hegel's schema, she simply *is*. The family, as the sphere of 'first nature,' confirms woman's bondage to nature as immediate and contin-gent and confirms her bondage to her husband as man gains a necessary connection to first nature through woman. The relation of woman to nature is significant because man's relation to nature is one of domina-tion: domination grounds objectification in the Hegelian schema and means the domination of some men by other men. But this domination of some men over other men includes the domination of all women.

In the preceding analysis of the pagan world we have relied on Hegel's interpretation of that world as suffering from a dualism in which first nature, as represented by woman in the family, is in conflict with reason, as represented by man in the state, such that the pagan world is doomed: there is no possibility of a reconciliation or *Aufhebung* of this conflict. Reason, as political life in the ancient world, is not truly universal in that it does not include particularity according to Hegel. As we see it, family life, in which male particularity is embedded, is created at woman's expense. She is tied to the immediate, has no particularity, and takes her revenge by acting as the agent of destruction of that world. As we turn to Hegel's account of the modern world we find that in the third part of the *Philosophy of Right*, published in 1821, Hegel has developed his concept of ethical life as man's 'second nature' more fully. In this work there is an explicit analysis of how Spirit objectifies itself as law, the state, and social and economic activity. The bifurcation of reason into familial and political, or particular and universal, that we find in the ancient world as described in the *Phenomenology*, becomes a triad composed of family, civil society, and state. The family is the sphere of the universal as undifferentiated unity; civil society represents the moment of particularity and the state is the sphere of universality in which the universal and particular are reconciled.

In the movement from family to civil society to the state, undifferentiated unity becomes differentiated universality or unity in difference.[23] In Spirit's movement toward universal self-knowledge the dualism which Hegel attributes to the pagan world is *aufgehoben* in the modern world. The economic activity which had been confined to the family and therefore to 'first nature' in the pagan world becomes a separate sphere of man's 'second nature' in the modern world as the sphere of civil society. And along with this development, Christianity, as the religion of freedom, emerges, making the true reconciliation or *Aufhebung* of first nature and second nature, particular and universal, possible. The revelation of God in Christ allows man to acquire the knowledge necessary to make the transition from an ethical life which is immediate and natural to one which is self-conscious and therefore truly universal.[24]

In the following analysis of the *Philosophy of Right* we shall show that the Hegelian schema with its tripartite structure and dialectical movement no more answers 'the woman question' than the pagan world did. The Hegelian world of man's 'second nature,' like the pagan world, is still made at woman's expense.

For Hegel, as we have seen, particularity must necessarily be incorporated into political life in order for that life to be truly universal but this does not mean that woman *qua* woman needs incorporation into the political sphere. Rather, he develops a philosophical system in the *Philosophy of Right* in which he conceives of particularity without the impediment of immediacy. Particularity and immediacy are separated and particularity is taken up into the male realm of civil society while woman remains trapped in the immediacy of the family.[25]

Hegel begins the section on ethical life in the *Philosophy of Right* with the family because 'the family is the logically prior society in as much as it represents the universal in its logically first moment of immediacy.' The family as the sphere of undifferentiated unity is said to be 'ethical (mind/spirit) in its natural or immediate phase'; there is an immediate identification of interests among the family members. But the moment of knowledge is the moment of mediation and withdrawal. Therefore one must leave the immediacy of the family to 'know' oneself; the family unity is thus negated when the (male) individuals emerge as particulars and move into civil society.

Civil society is the sphere of the particular, as distinct from the universal, and is composed of a plurality of male individuals each of whom pursues his own commercial and economic interests while endeavoring to satisfy his own particular needs and provide for his family. The individual interests and divergent needs are co-ordinated through the laws of political economy. Thus, in Hegel's developed political philosophy, the sphere of the principle of particularity is the sphere of civil society *not* the sphere of the family.

Alexandre Kojève claims that for Hegel the family is the sphere of particularity as opposed to the universality of the state but he concerns himself only with the *Phenomenology* and does not consider the *Philosophy of Right* where this problem is worked out in greater detail. As we have outlined above it is (male) civil society not the family that is the sphere of particularity in Hegel's later system. Since woman never leaves the family she never becomes a *consciously* particular self and the family represents, in the *Phenomenology*, only an unconscious sphere of particularity. Mary O'Brien, in her paper 'The Politics of Impotence,' claims that woman represents particularity in Hegel's system necessarily defeated by man as the agent of universality. But woman is the agent of destruction that defeats the universal male community in the pagan state. And, more importantly, the question of exactly *how* woman can represent particularity while never knowing herself as a particular being is a question that Hegel does not address and Kojève and O'Brien do not raise. To focus on the dualism of familial and political as Kojève does, or the dualism of sex as O'Brien does, is to slur over the more developed tripartite structure of the *Philosophy of Right* where the family represents the *universal* in its first moment of immediacy and male civil society, as the 'universal family,' is the sphere of conscious particularity.[26]

While Hegel believes that art, religion, and philosophy are the goals, or ultimate expressions, of humanity, he also believes that a proper state is necessary for their realization: the state is to mediate the conflicting interests of the possessive individualism of civil society. Thus, 'the state is the actuality of the ethical Idea' and the reconciliation of particular and universal occurs through the establishment of the state as a constitutional monarchy. While the universality of the state transcends family and civil society, Hegel nevertheless believes he has preserved both 'moments' in this form of government. The monarch preserves the 'moment' of the family since he inherits the right to rule through kinship or blood ties; and the estate structure of the government, by representing the different classes or estates of civil society, preserves the 'moment' of particularity. Hereditary monarchy means that the principle of the family moves from particularity in the *Phenomenology*, to 'love' in the first part of the *Philosophy of Right*, to 'blood' in the last analysis; but this movement to 'blood' as the principle of the family contradicts Hegel's claim that the *'true'* principle of the family as the sphere of immediacy is *love*.

When we consider the place of woman in this schema, we must return to the family because it is only here that we find woman. She does not enter civil society or the state.

The family is completed in three phases: (1) marriage, (2) family property and capital, and (3) the education of children, followed by the dissolution of the family. The family's bond of union is love, an 'immature' or 'immediate' form of reason. But an ethical marriage changes 'the natural sexual union ... into a union on the level of ... self-conscious love.'[27] This is a different situation from the one we encountered in the *Phenomenology* where love was not self-conscious. In the *Philosophy of Right*, the marriage contract eliminates the capricious subjectivism of love as sentiment and makes love the ethical 'moment' in marriage. For Hegel, the ethical unity which is present in the family is such that there is no distinction between what appears and what is: 'The family, as the immediate substantiality of mind, is specifically characterized by love, which is mind's feeling of its own unity. Hence, in a family one's frame of mind is to have self-consciousness of one's individuality within this unity as the absolute essence of oneself; with the result that one is not in it as an independent person but as a member.'[28] For two people in love with each other the meaning of each one's existence is revealed in the Other who is loved: the Other is the self and the self externalized. In the *Philosophy of Right* Hegel describes the union of love as having two moments: 'The first moment in love is that I do not wish to be self-subsistent and that, if I were, then I would feel defective and incomplete. The second moment is that I find myself in another person, that I count for something in the other, while the other in turn, comes to count for something in me.'[29]

If we consider this exposition on love in the light of the analysis of self-consciousness as the desire for recognition we find a critical inconsistency. While it is clear that love is a desire for recognition, for the lover desires the desire of the Other, the dialectic of love is not grounded in the hostility of a life-and-death struggle. And while the recognition in universal self-consciousness has transcended this initial struggle, recognition in a 'universal' sense is only possible between equals who know themselves to be free. In Hegel's philosophy I am myself only in distinguishing myself from the Other: since she is never consciously confronted in her particularity, woman never becomes an 'I'. Confined to the family and the dialectic of love woman lacks the negativity resulting from the initial sundering from nature and therefore never achieves an independent self-consciousness. She is never an equal Other and never knows herself to be free.

Only man 'dirempts' himself: only he struggles for recognition in the 'universal' sense. Woman remains within the family where only an abstract or undifferentiated identity can be achieved. Here, as in the *Phenomenology*, one would have to conclude that man can *truly* love only after he has created himself as a human being in the world outside the family. Since only *he* achieves a human existence only he can achieve truly human love.[30] Woman, confined to the dialectic of love, cannot truly love because she never creates herself as human in the world outside the family. Hegel's love relation cannot offer recognition in equality because it is not a relation where two individuals *recognize* each other in their individuality. It is not a relation where a man and a woman recognize each other *as* other. This presents us with a contradiction in that woman is defined in terms of love and yet cannot truly love. Since only man can achieve a truly human existence one would have to conclude that a truly *human* love is only possible between men! Jean Hyppolite in his *Studies on Marx and Hegel*, claims that 'the recognition which appears to be immediately forthcoming in love is open to the danger of foundering ... upon the lifeless in-itself.'[31] But it is not the love relation per se that causes this problem. It is male domination, as patriarchal rule, which confines woman to the immediate and does not allow her to become a self, an equal Other in Hegel's philosophy.

Hegel wants to insist that love is only possible between equals and implicitly claims that man and woman are equal in freedom. Thus woman *chooses* her subservience to man.[32] For Hegel, 'there can be no compulsion on people to marry,' and for the two people who wed, the marriage union 'is a self-restriction, but in fact it is their liberation, because in it they attain their substantive self-consciousness.' For him, 'our objectively appointed end and so our ethical duty is to enter the married state.' He defends the nuclear family against the rights of the extended family (what he calls 'family in the wide sense') and in this married state there is an 'identification of personalities, whereby the family becomes one person and its members become its accidents.' This he claims is the 'ethical mind/spirit' at work; what it means for woman is the total loss of self, for the 'one person' that the family becomes is *necessarily* the husband: 'The family as a legal entity in relation to others must be represented by the husband as head. Further, it is his prerogative to go out and work for its living, to attend to its needs, and to control and administer its capital.'[33]

But this is circular reasoning. The argument that the man *must be* the legal head of the family rests on the fact that he has the 'prerogative' to participate in public life and the woman does not. Woman has been assigned to the family and then told that she cannot have any authority here because she is not a public person. This assumption of male dominance in the patriarchal family, disguised by talk of the 'ethical mind/spirit' at work, precludes the kind of mutuality which Hegel conceives as the essence of marriage. Without a developed self-consciousness (grounded in the social and economic equality of the sexes), woman cannot meet man on the terrain of mutual recognition which love requires.

Hegel takes the socially conditioned 'given' of the bourgeois woman locked into family life and raises it to the level of 'essential nature.' In the *Philosophy of Nature* he writes: 'the male is the active principle, and the female is the receptive, because she remains in her undeveloped unity.'[34] Thus Hegel maintains both the Aristotelian and Christain bias concerning woman in all his works by making her a passive being who 'has her substantive destiny in the family, and to be imbued with family piety is her ethical frame of mind.'[35] And, while the logic of Hegel's system requires the tripartite structure of family, civil society, and state, the dialectical movement requires that the spheres of family and civil society be maintained or preserved as well as negated in the process of development toward the universality of the state. Therefore, woman 'becomes' the man whenever the family has any public appearance to make and she does the family 'maintenance' work required by the Hegelian dialectic. She maintains or 'preserves' the family while man moves into civil society and state. The spheres of man's second nature can be realized only if woman stays home to maintain the sphere of first nature.

In the *Philosophy of Right*, love is subordinated to the claims of marriage and reproduction, which in turn are subordinated to the claims of property. Within the Hegelian family, woman is in a state of absolute dependence on father and/or husband. It is not really a question of man and woman coming together in love, but rather marriage and the inheritance of property that are at issue. As Marcuse points out, the recognition which Hegel places at the beginning of the social order 'does not refer merely to the voluntary subordination ... of one person to another ... but to the justification of such recognition in the material sphere of society ... in the realm of appropriation and property, work and service, fear and discipline.'[36] 'Love' and 'ethics' mask the male domination of patriarchal rule and the essence of the family as property. Hegel's philosophy is ideological in its lack of an analysis of the difference between the working class and bourgeois family as well as in its patriarchal assumptions. Hegel says: 'The family, as person [read husband/father] has its real external existence in property; and it is only when this property takes the form of capital that it becomes the embodiment of the substantial personality of the family;' and 'the introduction of permanent property is linked with the introduction of marriage.' In and through the family, property is transformed from the 'arbitrariness of a single owner's particular need' to 'possessions specifically determined as permanent and secure.'[37] Hegel believes property to be essential for the realization of personal freedom. One must have property because consciousness is not simply inwardness; consciousness must externalize, move out from inwardness although ultimately it must turn back. Through property, as an externalization or going out of the self, a relation to nature as 'independent thinghood' is established which is one of mediation and objectification. Man expresses his freedom and gains historical continuity by acquiring a connection with things that do not have an internal life, by effectively appropriating and transmitting property through his family.

In order to realize the universality required by the socio-political spheres, property relations cannot be tied arbitrarily to the individual but must be established as a relation between the general community and the individual. Hegel believes that the right of inheritance of property through the family accomplishes the necessary connection between the general community and the individual, as well as establishing the ethicality of owning property, because the subject of property is the family as a unit. Therefore when one inherits family property one inherits property which, in principle, is communal.[38] The universality of this property is safeguarded in Hegel's system by limiting the arbitrariness of the freedom to bequeath it to others.

Within this Hegelian framework it seems that woman can own property during her lifetime but she cannot bequeath it to others. For all the talk of equality between husband and wife, it is the *husband* who distributes the family property. While a wife may divorce her husband and claim an equal share of the family property in the first part of Hegel's discussion, even when she divorces and gains property woman does not become truly human because she cannot effectively use the property, by transferring it to others, to express her humanity. Thus the ambiguity of woman's relation to property in Hegel's schema in the *Philosophy of Right* leaves woman deprived of the experiences of freedom and historical continuity which man gains through an ability not only to *own* property but to bequeath it to others.[39] Lest we worry too much over woman's claim to the family property, Hegel later tells us that while the family principle calls for the equality of inheritance, 'in the higher sphere of the state, a right of primogeniture arises together with estates rigidly entailed: it arises, however, not arbitrarily but as the inevitable outcome of the Idea of the state.'[40] So, the family is 'overreached' by the state in such a way that woman and all her children, except for the firstborn male, are denied the rights of inheritance.

According to Hegel, any social group that maintains its property by inheritance through the family not only protects family members from the arbitrary developments of civil society but guarantees that they will conduct themselves according to high ethical standards (since the family is the sphere of substantive ethical life). Thus, the aristocracy, because they receive their property through the right of primogeniture, are unusually fitted to hold positions as civil servants and political leaders. This argument, however, not only contradicts Hegel's view of property as something which can be freely disposed of by the owner but also makes nonsense of the idea of family solidarity since one of the male children inherits everything.[41] Through the right of primogeniture, property concerns 'infect' the family with the antagonisms of particularity that are supposed to be confined to civil society.

Clearly woman is not a free and equal Other (as lover) within the family. She is there to bear children: 'The relation of love between husband and wife is in itself not objective, because even if their feeling is their substantial unity, still their unity has no objectivity. Such an objectivity parents first acquire in their children in whom they can see *objectified* the entirety of their union.'[42] The relation of husband and wife is not inherently self-complete. They need the child. Marriage is for procreation and woman must become 'mother' so the family may achieve objective, explicit unity.

Hegel obscures his acceptance of male domination as patriarchal rule with talk of 'ethics' and 'love.' He writes: 'It must be noticed in connection with sex-relations that a girl in surrendering her body loses her honour. With a man, however, the case is otherwise, because he has a field for ethical activity outside the family. A girl is destined in essence for the marriage tie and for that only; it is therefore demanded of her that her love shall take the form of marriage and that the different moments of love shall attain their true rational relation to each other.'[43] Since woman has only one sphere in which to play out her entire existence she must not make any mistakes. If, however, the man should 'err' within this sphere he can always leave home and be 'ethical' in public.

Hegel wants to maintain that marriage is not a contractual relationship: it is a contract to transcend the standpoint of contract. He claims that the wedding as a public ceremony establishes the bond 'as something ethical, raised above the contingency of feeling and private inclination.' But why does this particular 'ethical' relationship require a public ceremony? Surely friendship is an ethical bond and yet it requires no public declaration or contract in the way marriage does. In fact, as Hegel himself has stated, civil society and the state offer all sorts of opportunities for ethical behaviour to the man, yet how many of these require a public ceremony to acknowledge their 'ethicality'?

While Hegel often masks his misogynist tendencies with a mystification that comes from his conception of woman as connected to 'first nature', it is not difficult to find all his prejudices revealed by his own words. First he says: 'The difference in the physical characteristics of the two sexes has a rational basis and acquires an intellectual and ethical significance ... Thus one sex is mind in its self-diremption into explicit personal self-subsistence and the knowledge and volition of free universality ... The other sex is mind maintaining itself in unity as knowledge and volition of the substantive ... It follows that man has his actual substantive life in the state, in learning and so forth, as well as in labour and struggle in the external world ... Woman, on the other hand, has her substantive destiny in the family.' Fortunately, the man can come home after a hard day of 'self-diremption' to the woman who offers him 'a tranquil intuition of ... unity': in this way man gains a connection to first nature through woman. Given the inadequacy of Hegel's account, one wonders what it is she receives in return. However, lest we wonder *why* she must remain at home Hegel details her limitations: 'Women are capable of education, but they are not made for activities which demand a universal faculty such as the more advanced sciences, philosophy and certain forms of artistic production. Women may have happy ideas, taste and elegance but they cannot attain to the ideal. The difference between men and women is like that between animals and plants. Men correspond to animals, while women correspond to plants because their development is more placid and the principle that underlies it is the rather vague unity of feeling. When women hold the helm of government, the State is at once in jeopardy, because women regulate their actions not by the demands of universality but by arbitrary inclinations and opinions. Women are educated – who knows how? – as it were by breathing in ideas, by living rather than acquiring knowledge. The status of manhood, on the other hand, is attained only by the stress of thought and much technical assertion.'[43] Thus we see that the limitation of woman's role in Hegel's philosophy comes from his own patriarchal prejudice, not woman's 'essential nature.' And, this patriarchal prejudice is supported by the actual division of 'feminine' and 'masculine' forms of education.[44]

In summary, we find that in the *Philosophy of Right* the bourgeois woman seems to be entitled to equal rights but when we look closely we see that she does not share the world equally with the bourgeois man in the Hegelian system. The identification of woman with first nature keeps woman 'in her place.' Just as first nature is the pre-condition for Spirit but is 'overreached' by Spirit, so the family is the pre-condition for the state but is overreached by the state. In the same way that mind/spirit 'overreaches' first nature, man's second nature 'overreaches' woman as keeper of first nature. The duality or bifurcation of nature applies to the roles that woman plays in Hegel's philosophy: she is 'person' and 'mother.' But Hegel's complicated schema which attempts to give woman as person equal rights in the sphere of second nature is 'overreached' by his conception of woman as mother, tied to first nature. When we look carefully we see that woman is bound to immediacy in the family precisely because she is in the marriage for purposes of procreation. In her case, second nature does not 'overreach' first nature and woman never achieves the level of an equal Other in Hegel's philosophy precisely because of her connection to first nature as mother. In preserving the sphere of the family through the bearing and rearing of children, woman must sacrifice her claim to self-consciousness. She has no contradiction between herself and first nature to negate – she lacks negativity because she remains confined within the sphere of 'mere animal life.' She can never aspire to concrete universality or individuality as an *Aufhebung* of particular and universal because she never achieves either particularity or universality. She is for others – not for herself.

The *Aufhebung* in which the family is maintained by woman on the level of feeling is not only at the expense of woman becoming an equal Other but at the expense of the ontogenetic principle. The progressive movement of Spirit towards universal self-consciousness which Hegel details in the *Phenomenology* is never recapitulated in woman. With the limitation of woman, there is a limitation of the system. Woman, like man, has the ability to reason and the capacity to act – to partake of second nature – yet she is limited to animal life. There is no possibility that the stages of Spirit will be repeated in woman. She can never aspire to 'concrete' universality, that is, individuality, since she cannot attain particularity much less universality. Hegel's universal is necessarily male and male is *not* universal. Humanity is both male and female and the claim to universality of human experience must allow for woman's experience and participation which Hegel's system does not. While Hegel is in search of a philosophical system which embraces all there is, his acceptance of male domination as patriarchal rule sets a limitation to his system such that a male rather than a human world is what is described.

All the significant Hegel scholars slide over 'the woman question' and do not succeed in recognizing the limitation that woman's place sets on his philosophy. Kojève, for example, finds it 'curious' that woman is the agent of destruction in the pagan world while Taylor writes off woman's role in the pagan world by saying that the ethical spirit goes under, 'in any case, by whatever exact steps.' Both miss the critical significance of woman's role which not only limits woman but limits Hegel's philosophy.[45]

The fundamental problem of woman and first nature, vis-à-vis man and second nature, is as unresolved in Hegel's philosophy as he shows it to be in the ancient pagan world: he is no more able to answer 'the woman question' than the ancients were. The reciprocal recognition between some men in the state of the ancient world relied upon the domination of some men by other men, and the domination of all woman. The modern world described by Hegel *still* rests on this domination and the concept of recognition depends upon woman not being capable of recognition. All the talk of equality obscures the basic inequality of Hegel's system in which recognition requires that there be someone who is not recognized. The tripartite structure of reason in the modern world, the movement of the Hegelian dialectic, and the process of recognition are all at woman's expense. Examining Hegel's work via 'the woman question' discloses Hegel's patriarchal bias, and raises the problem of whether or not the spheres to which woman has been assigned *can be* taken up and dialectically *aufgehoben*. If woman is given truly human status and not confined to immediacy and the family, then the family cannot be maintained or preserved as well as transcended in the Hegelian sense because this maintenance *requires* the denial of woman's humanity. And the denial of woman's humanity means that Hegel's system is unable to provide a true *Aufhebung* of the opposition between familial and non-familial, first nature and second nature, and woman and man. Thus, the structure upon which universal knowledge depends breaks down when we raise 'the woman question' and Hegel's system is shown to be incapable of achieving the universal knowledge it is striving for.

Hegel attempted to ground intersubjectivity in his treatment of recognition and the necessity of the Other for developed self-consciousness. However, the 'recognition' which is realized in civil society is the recognition of the atomic or possessive bourgeois individual. And since civil society is based on egoism, non-hostile recognition remains intact only in the restricted area of familial relations. But this 'recognition' is not truly reciprocal – it is at the expense of woman's consciousness of herself as a free and independent subject. Thus while Hegel shows that the family is a unique sphere of life with its own specific logic, nevertheless his patriarchal prejudice ultimately falsifies and obscures familial relations.

I wish to thank Ian Angus, Lorenne Clark, Steve Levine, and Mary O'Brien, all of whom provided impetus and inspiration for this paper.

NOTES AND REFERENCES

1 Ian Angus 'Instrumental Rationality and the New Left' unpublished paper, Toronto 1975, 1–2

2 Mary O'Brien 'The Politics of Reproduction' thesis, York University, Toronto, 1976, 2, 7, 211, 217

3 Richard J. Bernstein *Praxis and Action* (Philadelphia 1971) 14–24; Frederick Copleston S.J. *A History of Philosophy* VII pt 1 (Garden City 1963) 207–21; John Herman Randall jr *The Career of Philosophy* II (New York 1965) 300–5

4 Bernstein *Praxis* 14–24; Copleston *History* VII pt 1 207–21

5 Bernstein *Praxis* 23; Randall *Career* II 287, 301–3

6 Jean Hyppolite *Studies on Marx and Hegel* (New York 1969) 161–4

7 Ibid 26–8

8 Hegel *The Phenomenology of Mind* tr J.B. Baillie (New York 1967) 233

9 Ibid 234–7

10 Ibid 237

11 Hyppolite *Studies* 29, 163

12 Mary O'Brien 'The Politics of Reproduction' 45–56. I am indebted to Mary O'Brien's work in this thesis and in 'The Politics of Impotence' in J. King-Farlow and W. Shea eds *Contemporary Issues in Political Philosophy* (New York 1976) for my own analysis of Hegel.

13 Hegel *Phenomenology* 227

14 Alexandre Kojève *Introduction to the Reading of Hegel* ed Allan Bloom and tr James H. Nichols jr (New York 1969) 58

15 Hegel *Phenomenology* 470

16 J.N. Findlay *Hegel, A Re-Examination* (London 1958) 116–17; Kojève *Introduction* 60–1, 296–8; Charles Taylor *Hegel* (Cambridge 1975) 172–7

17 Kojève *Introduction* 61, 298

18 Hegel *Phenomenology* 476–7

19 Ibid 496

20 Kojève *Introduction* 62; Taylor *Hegel* 177

21 Hegel *Phenomenology* 498

22 The discussion of Hegel's philosophy of nature comes from my reading of Copleston *History* VII pt 1 238–42; Kojève *Introduction* 277; and Emil Fackenheim *The Religious Dimension in Hegel's Thought* (Boston 1970) 85–98, 110–11, 231, 270–1. Fackenheim introduces the concept of 'over-reach' in his interpretation of Hegel.

23 Copleston *History* VII pt 1 254

24 George Armstrong Kelly *Idealism, Politics and History* (Cambridge 1969) 345

25 This analysis of Hegel's position was clarified in a conversation with Ian H. Angus, September, 1977.
26 Kojève *Introduction* 60–1; Mary O'Brien 'The Politics of Impotence' unpublished, York University, 1974, 11a
27 *Hegel's Philosophy of Right* tr T.M. Knox (London 1967) 111 parag. 161
28 Ibid 110 parag. 158
29 Ibid 261
30 Kojève *Introduction* 244
31 Hyppolite *Studies* 162
32 O'Brien 'The Politics of Impotence' 154
33 *Philosophy of Right* 116 parag. 171
34 *Hegel's Philosophy of Nature* tr A.V. Miller (Oxford 1970) 413
35 *Philosophy of Right* 114 parag. 166
36 Herbert Marcuse *Studies in Critical Philosophy* tr Joris de Bres (Boston 1973) 108
37 *Philosophy of Right* 116 parags. 169, 170
38 Marcuse *Studies* 106
39 O'Brien 'The Politics of Reproduction' 19–20
40 *Philosophy of Right* 122
41 Shlomo Avineri *The Social and Political Thought of Karl Marx* (New York 1975) 27–9, 44
42 *Philosophy of Right* 263, addition to parag. 164
43 Ibid 114 parags. 165 and 166; 263, addition to parag. 164; and 263–4, addition to parag. 166
44 Michele LeDoeuff 'Women in Philosophy' *Radical Philosophy* 17 (Summer 1977) 3
45 Kojève *Introduction* 62; Taylor *Hegel* 177

Reproducing Marxist Man

MARY O'BRIEN

It has become fashionable in recent years to talk of a revival of Marxism. The most cursory examination of political activities over the past century demonstrates that Marxism has been a vital and immensely significant factor in political activity for at least that long, and that such a lively corpus of thought hardly needs reviving. However, as a consequence of the fact that the Marxist tradition in North America at the present time appears to rest mainly in the hands of some of the intelligentsia, whose commitment to class struggle pales beside their scramble for tenure in the universities, it is Marxist *theory*, and not Marxist practice, which has become respectable. Thus, the separation of theory and practice has also been successful, and now joins the other separations which Marx analysed as by-products of class struggle, the separation of head and hand, and of town and country, for example. This is serious, for Marx's notion of *praxis* as the strategic route to the achievement of rational and humane social relations in a creative and scientific unity of thinking and doing is enormously powerful and potentially effective. It also constitutes the most difficult of the tasks which Marx bequeathed to his followers.

Among those followers are a constituency on which perhaps the ruling classes had not reckoned. Marxism has had a significant impact on feminism. The reasons for this are fairly obvious. Marx is the philosopher par excellence of the oppressed, and women are oppressed. Marx is also the pre-eminent theorist of revolution, and even bourgeois feminism, however nervously, recognizes that the liberation of women is a revolutionary proposition, centring as it must upon the most venerable of social institutions, particularly upon family forms. Further, the determinant impact of economic factors on the condition of women has made Marx's critique of political economy particularly appealing. Women have also understood with varying degrees of precision the need for a feminist praxis, but it has not been entirely clear where the theoretical component of this praxis can be found. The most likely source is Engels, who proposed a theoretical model of the oppression of women which appears to unify the question of women's liberation with the dynamics of class struggle and the promise of the abolition of class division.[1] Finally, the compelling humanism of Marx's thought, considerably buttressed recently by the translation and publication of his early works, has widened the appeal of his later and quite dauntingly complex works.

Despite these factors, there is increasing evidence that the promise of a feminist Marxism has become problematic.[2] There are fairly obvious reasons for this. The experience of women after Marxist revolutions, especially in the Soviet Union, has not been especially encouraging.[3] A change in the ownership of the means of production obviously does not produce a reflex qualitative transformation in the relations of women to men. Many women are beginning to wonder if the Marxist inheritance, which can offer a correct analysis of economic depression, can also offer an adequate theoretical perspective from which to view the present and the tradition which I have elsewhere called 'male-stream thought.'[4] This philosophical heritage is shot through with the ideology of male supremacy, and Marx is indubitably a thinker within this tradition, however original and however brilliant. Marx's inclusion of women's oppression in the general oppression of class division is, perhaps, inadequate. Women's oppression is qualitatively different from class oppression, and the qualitative differentiation which must be made in the first instance in theoretical terms simply does not emerge from Marx's work in a direct way.

These difficulties have surfaced both in feminist activism and in feminist scholarship, which are not wholly estranged. Women have recognized the need for the unification of knowledge which lurks under such cumbersome labels as 'inter-disciplinary Women's Studies.' The social sciences, for example, have produced data which orthodox Marxism has had difficulty in assimilating; perhaps psychoanalysis is the prime case, with its provocative and controversial theory of femininity. With some unorthodox exceptions Marxists have been suspicious of Freudians, and feminists have tended to choke on penis envy.[5] Yet psychoanalytical insights have enriched understanding of some of those areas which have caused most difficulty for feminist analysis. Wilhelm Reich, for example, argued that psyches which developed under the sweeping patriarchal authoritarianism of czarist Russia could not be transformed by a simple assertion that the family was officially defunct, or by merely superficial changes in the external conditions of family life.[6]

Psychology has much to offer in the area of gender identity, just as sociology has much to offer in the area of gender socialization. The hostility between Marxist social science, which seems largely to have found its critical capital in the workplace, and 'bourgeois' social science, perceived only as an exercise in ideological manipulation, is a hostility which feminists must examine in a critical way. Women need not neglect the psycho-social dimensions of male supremacy and the sociology of the family with the cavalier disparagement in which vulgar economist determinisms present themselves as the totality of a 'Marxist' social science.

The examination and criticism of these difficulties need not cow us, and we do not need to retreat before the possibility that the difficulties may emerge from defects in Marx's own theoretical understanding. There are few sharper historical ironies than the posthumous conversion of Marx the iconoclast, that most trenchant critic of ideological modes of understanding, into some kind of ahistorical saint whose work is perceived in canonical terms. In this paper, I want to open a critical examination of the marginality and inadequacy of Marx's understanding of reproduction; I then want to note the historical specificity of these defects, and to give some indication as to why a dialectical, historical, and materialist critique, derived from but superseding Marxist theory, offers the most promising ground for the development of a truly feminist praxis.

Marx, following upon the work of Hegel, grappled with the proposition that all reality is *process*. Process is understood as the form of all development and all interaction between the human world and the natural world. Process in this first instance is an abstract expression of the reality of action, thought, and experience, bringing the tumultuous and crowded contents of human history into a dynamic theoretical perspective. At the same time, process represents a concrete unity of humanity and the natural world, a unity born in struggle to meet and overcome the constrictions of necessity.

This sort of approach to socio-historical understanding is one to which feminism is at once sympathetic. The separation of 'Man' from nature may be perceived as the source, for example, of such problems as environmental erosion and the mindless triumphs of technocracy, which many feminists understand as related to masculine perceptions of power.

Women are also aware that within the tradition of masculine under-standing of the 'natural' world there is a significant gender differentia-tion. Men are somehow separate from and in an antagonistic relation to Nature, while women are in some even vaguer sense unified and indeed imprisoned by Nature. Hegel and Marx were both concerned to reinstate the notion of a synthesis of human and natural worlds, a concern born of the Enlightenment's over-confident proclivity to perceive man and nature as eternally at war, with man's progress being marked rather spe-cifically by his ability to overcome and control nature. Such a synthesis could not be brought about, Hegel and Marx realized, by wilfully impos-ing a 'natural' or metaphysical harmony upon the man/nature dialectic which ignored the empirically disharmonious historical reality of this relation. What both thinkers tried to capture was the *form* of historical process in a way which did not preclude the diversity and struggle which constitute the content of history. The mode of the analysis which Hegel conceived of and Marx nurtured was of course the dialectical method.

There is no easy way into the notion of the science of dialectics. Here, however, we might pause with Hegel for a moment for two relevant reasons.[7] One is that Hegel recognized, somewhat imperfectly, that the process of human biological reproduction is, as an instance of process in general, dialectically structured. The other is that a brief examination of the way in which Hegel examined the process sheds useful if still crude light on the meaning of dialectics. We have, in the process of reproduc-tion, the coming together of two opposites, the male and female 'seeds.' This synthesis is brought about by human action, and the particularity of each parent is destroyed, or, in the terminology of dialectics, negated. However, this unity which is a negation in the first instance, grows and expands until it bursts forth into the historical world as something new and different but undoubtedly real. The act of birth in turn cancels out the negativity inherent in the seed, for the child is not only a new par-ticularity; he is potentially universal, both potential man and potential Man, both individual and, to use young Marx's phrase, species-being.[8] *HE* is this synthesis of universal and particular, ready to play his part in the Hegelian drama in which Reason is objectified in the world through human praxis.

Hegel's very astute observation of the dialectical structure of repro-duction does not carry human affairs out of the animal into the social realm. This is because he sees this process as devoid of the self-directed workings of a true and rational self-consciousness: birth is pre-rational and therefore in an odd sense always pre-historical. Hegel, who notes correctly that human labour is the activity which mediates between people and nature, does not regard the labour of childbirth as philosophically significant. In fact, the only 'labour' involved in reproductive process is copulation, which is at least a novel view of that process, but it is *mindless* labour, informed by passion rather than reason.[9] Hegel is, of course, a profound mysogynist, who sees women as a disruptive and irrational historical force, asserting the value of individual life over the greater rational value of world-historical life. Obsessed with the curious reluctance to have their children killed, women stand in the way of Man's historic destiny, which consists of the eternal need to do death-dealing battle with other men, thus defying enslavement to the Great Negation, death itself, and asserting the value of the community over the mere life of the individual. The real cause of Hegel's denial of a reproductive consciousness, however, lies in his view of reproduction as wholly organic and pre-rational. For Hegel, patriarchy is both natural and pre-historical.

Hegel's discovery of the dialectical structure of biological reproduction, however imperfect, is a useful one. We also note that it was not part of the Hegelian baggage which Marx appropriated and transformed in the development of materialist dialectics. Marx is more humanely concerned with the oppression of women than Hegel was, but his understanding of the historical significance of the family hovers mistily on the edge of his insight into the historical forms of class struggle. Seeking to specify the historical conditions under which men might take rational control of the productive necessities imposed by their daily need to 're-produce' themselves, Marx never comes to terms with the social relations of reproduction in anything other than a reflexive way.

He accepts uncritically Proudhon's view of the condition of women: as men work historically to liberate themselves, history will somehow liberate women as a bonus. Women are therefore passive beneficiaries, with the additional usefulness of presenting a rough quantitative measure of how the class struggle is coming along. Further, Marx, who so expanded upon Hegel's insight into the mediative and creative powers of human labour, shares Hegel's astigmatism as to the fact that women *labour* to produce children. We do not, of course, argue that productive labour and reproductive labour are the same thing.[10] We do argue that reproductive labour cannot simply be ignored, as is the case with the two thinkers we are talking about, and in fact is the case with 'male-stream' thought in general.

Birth is not an object of philosophy – Marxist man, impressively human as he is, somehow never gets born. This neglect of any systematic analysis of reproductive labour is very important. It is by the unification of labour and thought, of theory and practice, that men make history, and in so doing they continuously transform and make the world and transform and make themselves. It is, further, this praxis which ultimately cancels the opposition between men and nature. Labour, together with rational consciousness of what one is doing when one works, mediates this opposition, integrating each man with his world and ensuring that men understand themselves as historical activists.[11] For Hegel, work is the animator of self-consciousness and its possibilities of universality, the progression from particular man to the unification of Man in general. For Marx, labour is the route to true consciousness, the consciousness which recognizes the collective need to resist the alienation and exploitation inherent in class antagonism and irrational modes of production.

It is not intended here to deny Marx's compelling analysis of the creative and transformative powers of productive labour. Likewise, Marx never denied that women, too, might develop a true consciousness and participate in the class struggle. However, one result has been a belief that the possibility of women participating in their own liberation depends upon their participation as workers in the productive realm, a view which has become increasingly problematic. We therefore note that the neglect of a serious analysis of reproductive labour short-changes the notion of labour as mediator between the social and human worlds, and tends to perpetuate Marx's error in subsuming gender struggle in class struggle. Perceived as accidental and irrational, the act of giving birth has no power to constitute a socio-historical world, but remains brute, dumb, and intransigent. The fact that genetic continuity is in some sense a material base of human history goes unnoticed and, more importantly, in all the efforts to analyse the determinants of human consciousness, the notion of such a phenomenon as *reproductive consciousness* is not seriously entertained. As it does not exist in a meaningful way, reproductive consciousness does not have to look for its own roots or analyse its own properties, and the ground of the social relations of reproduction are not sought in the process of reproduction. In Hegel's case, they are sought in affective and spiritual life; in Marx's case, they are assumed to be by-products of the dominant mode of production.

Marx's socio-historical model thus suffers from a real ambiguity as to the status of the family, which is, of course, the historical form in which the social relations of reproduction are most commonly realized. Marx's formal 'model' consists of a substructure which has as its content a historically specific and generalized mode of production and the forms of class struggle which have created it, define it, and will ultimately abolish it. This substructure of historical process determines the forms of such social institutions as law, literature, religion, and politics, which reflect the needs and values of the dominant class. The use of such differentiated words as 'determine' and 'reflect' is deliberate, for the actual workings of the relations between the economic substructure and the social constituents of what Marx calls the superstructure, or, sometimes, the infrastructure, were never worked out in detail. There are some hints that a key role is played by the political infrastructure, both in terms of providing a power base for ruling class self-conservation and in terms of the transformation of the ideologies of conflicting classes into real struggle. The important question about the model here, however, concerns the location and relations of the family. The answer is by no means clear. In some places – in the *Communist Manifesto*, for example – the family is treated as a superstructural phenomenon which reflects its market substructure in the reduction of marriage to a set of property relations in which female bodies become commodities, a fate which male bodies somehow escape.[12] Male bodies, insofar as they incorporate labour power, are commodities in the labour market, but in the marital marketplace men are traders. While Marx is savagely satirical on the subject of bourgeois marriage, he makes no claim for more progressive relations among the proletariat, though in other places he waxes a little sentimental on this subject.[13] He certainly does not see the opposition of male-female as the ground of historical transformation.

The ambiguity of reproduction is even more pronounced in Engels' account of the economic origins of male supremacy and what he is pleased to call, with a fine Hegelian flourish, 'the world-historical defeat of the female sex.'[14] Engels begins by placing reproduction firmly in the substructure of the historical model: production and reproduction jointly constitute *necessity*, which is the reason why the substructure is the determinant realm in the first place. However, having argued that both production and reproduction are necessary and substructural, Engels goes on to argue that family forms are economically determined. To object to this is not theoretical hair-splitting: it is precisely the historical development of rational means for dealing with necessity which embodies the Marxist vision of a humane and classless future, but evidently only one pole of the axis of necessity can be dealt with. Necessity has two poles, production and reproduction, but in Engels' model production subsumes reproduction, for the relations of production alone leave scope for human praxis.

Thus Engels argues that the development of private property brought about a great deal of uncomfortable disorder in societies in which matrilineal kinship had constituted both a mode of historical continuity and a determinate series of social arrangements. Property 'made the man's position in the family more important than the woman's.'[15] Property thus brought about one of the greatest revolutions of all time but, according to Engels, it was a peaceful one. Women did not resist these changes, the only reason which Engels offers being that they were delighted with the institution of patriarchal marriage, which saved them from the unpleasantness of a variety of sexual partners.[16] Sex is, for women, a distasteful necessity from which the fine Victorian sensibilities of Engels and Marx would feign protect them. In any case, the women of ancient times contemplated this major revolution with equanimity and passivity, and a 'simple decree sufficed that in the future the offspring of the male members should remain within the gens,' and property could thus be secured to male inheritance. Engels was writing after Marx's death but there is no reason to suppose that Marx would have disagreed. Both men had read Morgan, and Engels quotes one of Marx's marginal notes on the Morgan text to the effect that the transition from mother right to father right 'in general ... seems to be the most *natural* transition'[17] (my italics).

Here we must face the fact that in this area Marx is a true bud of the great tree of traditional 'male-stream' thought. He is as ambiguous on the central question of the nature of Nature as his predecessors have been since classical philosophers first grappled with the question. Nature evidently suffers from the same kind of contradictory characteristics which her daughters exhibit; she is the mother of and partakes of the nature of Eve and the Blessed Virgin. Fecund and providential on the one hand, she is unpredictable and wantonly destructive on the other. She is in one sense the source of human nature, but has exasperatingly concealed in the fearful crevices of her mysterious womb just exactly what that human nature is. She demands conformity with her own nature while mocking man, her creature, with a denial of any immediate knowledge of the meaning of the natural.

Marx, of course, does not sail on these speculative ontological seas, but, as R. Pascal has noted, he is inconsistent in his application, for example, of the term *Naturwüchsig* (growing naturally).[18] In *The German Ideology* he uses this phrase to denote pre-capitalist economic forms in which labour is divided by 'natural predispositions,' such as strength, need, and other accidental factors. This sort of arrangement produces what Marx calls 'natural' capital, which remains attached to the guilds whose labours produced it in the first place. Elsewhere, Marx speaks of 'natural' society in terms of cleavage between particular and collective interests, an opposition which creates class differentiation and a loss of the control of the product of labour. Over against this 'natural' society Marx poses communist society which has regained control of the social product by means of rational planning.

Pascal does not offer an analysis of the roots of this inconsistency, but it is important that this be done. This kind of ambiguity is not random, but is related to a much more radical defect in Marx's model which never solves the problem of the relation of the two poles of natural necessity, production and reproduction. Marx wants to develop a theoretical model which transcends the idealist speculations of former models, especially that of Hegel. His historical dialectics are to be materialist dialectics, which must avoid rootless metaphysic on the one hand and the grounded realities of Lockean sense perception on the other. At the same time, of course, Marx must retain the integrity of both mental life and empirical reality. His model therefore attempts to ground history in natural necessity, perceived as a determinate but not completely determinant substructure of all human endeavour, for necessity commands both action and reflection and human praxis is creative and versatile.

The postulate that men must eat is rescued by Marx from proverbial crudity to its proper status as the a priori of individual life, while the postulate that men must *produce* to eat becomes for him the a priori of social life. Thus Marx talks continuously of the need for men to 'reproduce' themselves, and by this he almost always means reproduction of the self on a daily basis by the continual and necessary restoking of the organism with fuel for its biological needs. Man makes himself materially, and this is of course true. Man, however, is also 'made' reproductively by the parturitive labour of women, but Marx ultimately combines these two processes. This has the effect of negating biological continuity, which is mediated by women's reproductive labour, and replacing this with productive continuity in which men, in making themselves, also make history. Marx never observes that men are in fact separated *materially* from both nature and biological continuity by the alienation of the male seed in copulation.

This negation of the human significance of biological reproduction is quite specific. Like Hegel, Marx deals with the question as a young man, and, also like Hegel, he appears to be more concerned with the question of sexuality than with the understanding of the social significance of reproductive process, of which sexuality is but a part. In the Third of the *1844 Manuscripts*, Marx introduces the question of sexual relations in an exemplary way, signifying the thoughtlessness with which crude communism wreaks indiscriminate social destruction in a mindless passion for making all private property communal property: 'Finally, this tendency to oppose general private property to private property is expressed in an animal form: *marriage* (which is incontestably a form of *exclusive private property*) is contrasted with the community of women, in which women become communal and common property. One may say that this idea of the *community* of women is the *open secret* of this entirely crude and unreflective communism. Just as women are to pass from marriage to universal prostitution, so the whole world of wealth (i.e., the objective being of man) is to pass from the relation of exclusive marriage with the private owner to the relation of universal prostitution with the community.'[19]

Marx appears to see that his broad castigation of both bourgeois marriage and communal sex may be a little sweeping, so he goes on to try to strip away from the 'open secret' – a simple and primitive lust and resentful envy – some of its secrecy: 'In the relationship with *woman*, as the prey and handmaid of communal lust, is expressed the infinite degradation in which man exists for himself; for the secret of this relationship finds its *unequivocal*, incontestable, *open* and revealed expression in the relation of man to woman and in the way in which the *direct* and *natural* species relationship is conceived. The immediate, natural and necessary relation of human being is also the *relation* of *man* to *woman*. In this *natural* species relationship man's relation to nature is directly his relation to man, and his relation to man is directly his relation to nature, his own *natural* function. Thus, in this relation is *sensually revealed*, reduced to an observable *fact*, the extent to which human nature has become nature for man and to which nature has become human nature for him.'[20]

The almost indecent haste with which a relation of man to woman becomes a relation of man to man is perhaps exacerbated in translation, for English, unlike German, does not provide separate words for masculine man (*man*) and mankind (*mensche*). Giving Marx the broadest possible latitude we may interpret him as saying: the immediate natural and necessary human relationship is that of men and women. In this relationship people are conscious of their own sexual need, which is the need for another human being. This need confirms them as both natural and social beings, and the degree to which they can create humane conditions for the expression of this relationship is an indicator of how far they have progressed from mere animality. Such an interpretation proclaims an important truth, that sexual relations are not only necessary, but necessarily social, which is not, interestingly, true of the need to produce.

In a primitive state, individuals could theoretically pluck only their own fruits from the tree of life; the race, of course, would not then survive. Despite this, or perhaps because of this, Marx joins traditional philosophy in denying to birth any specifically human significance. The ground of Marx's version of this persistent tenet of male supremacist ideology is that any man who owes his existence to another is a 'dependent being,' and is thus precluded from free expression of his humanity: 'But I live completely by another person's favour when I owe to him [sic] not only the continuance of my life but also *its creation*; when he is its *source*. My life has necessarily such a cause outside itself if it is not my own creation. The idea of *creation* is thus one which it is difficult to eliminate from popular consciousness. This consciousness is *unable to conceive* that nature and man exist on their own account, because such an existence contradicts all the tangible facts of practical life.'[21]

Marx appears to share the Greek notion that the male is 'true parent' of the child without recognizing the prejudice inherent in this formulation.[22] Furthermore, he seems quite unperturbed by the positing of a 'material' view of a fundamental life process which 'contradicts all the facts of practical life.' He is interested, of course, in man's historical, self-made nature. Yet in asserting this, he quite specifically negates reproductive continuity, which he sees as infinite regress lurking as progress. If, like Aristotle, he argues, you say that man is produced by the coitus of two human beings, you lapse into infinite progression (who engendered my grandfather and his father and so forth) and do not keep in mind 'the *circular movement* which is perceptible in that progression, according to which man, in the act of generation reproduces himself: thus *man* always remains the subject.'[23]

Marx is aware of the essential sociability of reproduction and of temporal problems within the process. He does not, however, analyse the nature of the temporal problem, which is specifically a *male* problem. Male participation in the continuum of species-being ends with the alienation of the male seed. Male time-consciousness is thus discontinuous. For women, species continuity is confirmed by reproductive labour.

Marx, not having analysed the dialectics of reproductive process, does not see this. A stubborn insistence that biological continuity *is* continuity, he says, can only lead to the question of who created man in the first place, a 'perverted' and 'abstract' question which posits non-existence. The young Marx, still engaged in 'hating all gods,' the passion which had informed his doctoral dissertation, simply takes refuge in polemic at this point: 'Ask yourself whether that progression exists as such for rational thought. If you ask a question about the creation of nature and man you abstract from nature and man. You suppose them *non-existent* and you want me to demonstrate that they *exist*. I reply: give up your abstraction and at the same time you abandon your question. Or else, if you want to maintain your abstraction, be consistent, and if you think of man and nature as non-existent think of yourself too as non-existent, for you are also man and nature. Do not think, do not ask me any question, for as soon as you think and ask questions your *abstraction* from the existence of nature and man becomes meaningless. Or are you such an egoist that you conceive everything as non-existent and yet want to exist yourself?'[24]

Socialist man, on the contrary, takes *his* proofs of his man-made existence from real experience, the implication being that getting born is not real experirence, and giving birth even less so. Marx is overly excited, because the question that he raises is not the one which needs to be asked at all. We must ask Marx what is wrong with biological reproduction as a basis of real continuity. Of course people 'make themselves' in their interaction with the world and other people, but why can socialist man not be created until birth has been deprived of the capacity to create continuity? Marx could quite easily have posited a dynamic *dialectic* between biological time and historical time without lapsing into the trap of the infinite regression of crude causality. He did not do so, for he did not recognize that reproductive process is dialectical, or that the social relations of reproduction and the ideologies of male supremacy are determined by reproductive rather than productive process.

This is not the mere aberration of a young thinker. The transfer of reproductive power and sociability to productive relations remains constant. In *The German Ideology*, Marx is less confused, but he still insists on the hegemony of productive labour in the formation of human historical consciousness, a position from which he never retreats. In the discussion of biological reproduction in *The German Ideology* he seems at first sight to be presenting us with the remarkable spectacle of people eating and producing and needing before they are born at all: 'life involves before everything else eating and drinking' while the second determination of life process emerges from the fact that needs produce more needs 'and this production of new needs is the first historical act': 'The third circumstance which from the very first, enters into historical development is that men, who daily remake their own life, begin to make other men, to propogate their kind: the relation between man and wife, parents and children, the FAMILY. The family which to begin with is the only social relationship, becomes later, when increased needs create new social relations and the increased population new needs, a subordinate one.'[25]

Here, Marx backtracks a little from 'before everything else'; these are not to be seen as stages of development, he says, but as aspects of development which exist simultaneously, and production and reproduction appear as a double relationship; on the one hand natural, on the other social. At this point Marx *negates* the sociability and historicism of reproductive relations: 'It follows from this that a certain mode of production ... is always combined with a certain mode of cooperation.' It also follows that reproduction also involves a certain mode of co-operation, but Marx does not say so. Only production thereafter forms consciousness, and production, by an unexplained alchemy, also forms the social relations of reproduction.

In *Capital*, Marx has made up his mind on the question of what constitutes a natural economy, and he has also abandoned the radically liberal individualism which produced the youthful hysteria evident in his diatribe against the dependence of life on the activity of others. In his discussion of commodity fetishism, he defines 'the particular and natural form of labour' as that in which the personal interdependence of the members of the economic unit is present to consciousness in its true social form.[26] For an example of this directly associated labour form, Marx tells us, we do not need to go back to 'that spontaneously developed form which we find on the threshold of the history of all civilized races.' We still have examples of this 'spontaneous' form close to hand, for we can find it 'in the *patriarchal* industries of a peasant family' (my italics). Marx presumably feels that the patriarchal family had developed 'spontaneously' and without struggle, presumably having in mind 'the simple decree' of which Engels speaks. The family, ancient or modern, 'possesses a spontaneously developed system of division of labour.'[27] As we saw, even the postulation of an ancient matriarchate did not sully the spontaneity of patriarchal naturalness.

One of the reasons for Marx's position, apart from the uncriticized dominance of the dogma of male supremacy which was specific to his epoch, is that he is preoccupied with the notion of universality, which he pulls down from idealist heights and represents as real co-operative sociability. Sociability and co-operation are the pre-conditions of class-less society, and Marx wants to demonstrate that universality – perceived as the annulment of alienation and the restoration of a unity of men with nature, with their products and with other men – is the goal of history and the condition of human freedom. He therefore seeks experiential 'universals' and finds eating and sexuality. However, he perceives the latter as immediate, while the former requires the mediation of produc-tion. The labour of reproduction is excluded from the analysis, and not only because children appear spontaneously. Reproductive labour, thus sterilized, does not produce value, does not produce needs and therefore does not make history or make men. Birth as such is contingent, immedi-ate, and uninteresting, a 'subordinate' relationship.

What is missing is an analysis of reproductive process, for such an analysis immediately shows a significant form of alienation; the alienta-tion of the male seed. Marx's notion of the origins of class struggle could just as easily and plausibly describe the origins of gender struggle: 'Every self-alienation of man, from himself and from nature, appears in the relation which he postulates between other men and himself and nature ... In the real practical world this self-alienation can only be expressed in the real, practical relation of man to his fellow men. The medium through which alienation occurs is itself a *practical* one. Through alienated labour, therefore, man not only produces his relation to the object and to the process of production as to alien and hostile men; he also produces the relation of other men to his production and his product, and the relation between himself and other men. Just as he creates his own pro-duction as a vitiation, a punishment, and his own product as a loss, as a product which does not belong to him, so he creates the domination of the non-producer over production and its product. As he alienates his own activity, so he bestows upon the stranger an activity which is not his own.'[28]

The origin of the struggle between men and women rests upon a simi-lar process. The child is alienated from the man, for any man can have fathered this child. Paternity, unconfirmed by human labour, remains an *idea*. History shows us that men have not simply suffered this alienation and loss of continuity. They have done something about it, actions which require social relations between men which are cooperative – you leave my woman alone and I'll do the same for you – and relations between men and women which are appropriative and therefore relations of dominance. Men annul the alienation of the seed and give social substance to the idea of paternity by the act of appropriating children. This act is at the same time the act of appropriating the alienated reproductive labour power of the mother. Here lies a relation of brotherhood between men of all classes which has nothing to do with modes of production, and everything to do with the necessities embedded in reproductive dialectics.

The importance of Marx's failures in understanding the complexities of Necessity is a failure which can best be understood in terms of Marx's own work. Men, Marx tells us, can only confront the problems which history presents to them. Just as the dialectics of class struggle did not become clear enough to permit systematic theoretical formulation of their internal logic until industrial development had reached a certain stage, so too, the dialectics of reproduction must await a maturity which did not exist in Marx's lifetime. The mediate agent of maturity in each case is the same: technological development. Only in the epoch of potentially universal contraception can the history of gender struggle be theoretically grasped. Only in this era does such a notion as rational control of reproduction become thinkable. Such control is hardly imminent. Humanity has had at hand the possibility of rational control of production for some time, yet the inhuman fetishisms of commodity production persist. Further, the dialectical analysis of reproduction does not offer instant freedom for women. What it does mean is that women have now to do what men did aeons ago: come to terms with their altered reproductive consciousness.

The fact that paternity is not immediate means that the discovery of paternity was at some distant time a historical event. As a relation of non-immediate cause and effect, the discovery of paternity must await a certain quite advanced stage of the development of the human intellect. Even then, paternity remains ideal and problematic. Paternity represents a double freedom for men: a freedom from labour and a freedom to accept or reject the child. The appropriation of the child cancels paternal alienation from species continuity, but it is the appropriation of a helpless creature, and therefore entails certain responsibilities. Likewise, men are placed in opposition to one another as possible potencies, and are forced into social relations to deal with this problem.

The freedom which women gain from the second historical transformation in reproductive process, the development of contraceptive technology, is equally problematic. This technology can be abused in a number of ways, and we already see signs of attempts to solve the tensions embedded in capitalism's recent reversal from a pro-natal, expansionist population policy to a curb on the politically dangerous people in the third world. There are also indications that advanced automation in developed countries is producing a larger industrial reserve army of unemployed than capitalism can easily manipulate. These are probably the reasons why the necessary resources to develop universal contraception were allocated in the first place. It was unlikely that this was done with the intention of creating women as the progressive force in history which they now, somewhat benumbed, find themselves to be. In fact, the allocation of resources has been minimal, and has stopped well short of a safe and sophisticated contraceptive technology which a humane rationality demands, but the labour needs of capitalism do not.

Despite these problems, and many more, history cannot be turned back. The social relations of reproduction are changing and will change more. The question is how much control people can have over these transformations. Marx's great strength is that his theory and method permit us to begin to go to work on these problems. The process of reproduction is historical, material, and dialectical, and can be subjected to critical analysis on those terms. What does have to be done is a modification of Marx's socio-historical model, which must now account for two opposing substructures, that of production and that of reproduction. This in fact improves the model. The institutions and ideologies which Marx describes as superstructural are in fact *mediative*. They mediate the oppositions both within and between the social relation of production on the one hand and the social relations of reproduction on the other. This is a very crude formulation, and the uses, refinements, and implications of such a model remain to be worked out. This is an urgent task for feminism, but one at least made possible by the theoretical rigour which is Marx's bequest to us.

NOTES AND REFERENCES

1 Lewis Henry Morgan *Ancient Society* (1877; rpt New York 1963); Engels *The Origin of the Family, Private Property, and the State* tr E.B. Leacock (New York 1973). Marx made an abstract of ancient society to which Engels had access, and which can be found (in Russian) in *Marx-Engels Archives* ix (1941) 1–192.

2 Joining the call for a feminist revision of Marxist theory are Eleanor Burke Leacock (in her Introduction to Engels *Origin* 46), Sheila Rowbotham, Juliet Mitchell and, indirectly, Simone de Beauvoir.

3 There is a fairly extensive literature on this subject. See, for example,
V.S. Dunham 'Sex: From Free Love to Puritanism' in A. Inkeles and K.
Geiger eds *Soviet Society: A Book of Readings* (London 1961); H.K. Geiger *The
Family in Soviet Russia* (Cambridge, Mass. 1968); I. de Palencia *Alexandra
Kollontay* (New York 1941); W. Reich *The Sexual Revolution* (New York
1971); Hilda Scott *Does Socialism Liberate Women?* (Boston 1975).

4 Mary O'Brien 'The Politics of Impotence' in J. King-Farow and W. Shea
eds *Contemporary Issues in Political Philosophy* (New York 1976)

5 The anti-Freud polemic launched by Betty Friedan in *The Feminist Mystique* (New York 1963) has given way to the more subtle appraisals of, for
example, Juliet Mitchell in *Woman's Estate* (New York 1973). The unification of the social sciences and the fusion of Marx and Freud are by no
means specifically feminist objectives. Some such endeavour colours the
scholarly practice of the critical theorists of the so-called Frankfurt School
and is important, too, to much French existentialist thought.

6 Wilhelm Reich *The Sexual Revolution* especially 182–90

7 The detailed analysis appears in the fragment 'On Love' in Hegel *Early
Theological Writings* tr T.M. Knox (Chicago 1948) 305–7.

8 'On Love' 303–5. A very important early work on the family, *The System
of Ethical Life*, has recently been translated by T.M. Knox and H.S. Harris,
and has been accepted for publication by SUNY Press.

9 Hegel's view of copulation as a form of work can be found in *The System
of Ethical Life* tr Knox and Harris. I am much indebted to Professor Harris
for his permission to quote from this important translation.

10 For a discussion of this differentiation, see Mary O'Brien 'The Politics of
Reproduction' doctoral dissertation, York University, Toronto, 1976.

11 'What distinguishes the worst architect from the best of bees is this, that
the architect raises his structure in imagination before he erects it in
reality ... By thus acting on the external world and changing it, he at the
same time changes his own nature'; Marx *Capital* I (Moscow 1954) pt III
ch VII 174. Reproductive labour might be said to combine the functions of
the architect and the bee: like the architect, parturitive woman knows
what she is doing; like the bee, she cannot help what she is doing. But a
new life changes the world and the consciousness of the woman.

12 Marx and Engels *The Communist Manifesto* (New York 1955) 27–9

13 Engels, perhaps, more so: see for example, the touching tale of Jack and
Mary in Engels *The Condition of the Working Class in England* (London
1969) 173–4. Juliet Mitchell quotes Marx's early work ('Chapitre de
Mariage' *Œuvres Completes* ed Molitor *Œuvres Philosophiques* I 25) in
which Marx speaks of the 'sanctification of the sexual instinct' as 'the
spiritual essence of marriage' (Juliet Mitchell *Woman's Estate* 110).

14 Engels *Origin* 120
15 Ibid 119
16 Eleanor Burke Leacock, in her Introduction (ibid 7–57), notes Engels' Victorian bias: 'women should by nature value chastity.'
17 Ibid 120
18 Marx and Engels *The German Ideology* ed R. Pascal (New York 1947) 291–2n
19 Marx 'Economic and Philosophical Manuscripts' tr T.B. Bottomore in Erich Fromm ed *Marx's Concept of Man* (New York 1970) 125
20 Ibid 126
21 Ibid 138
22 'The mother is no parent of that which is called her child, but only nurse of the new-planted seed that grows. The parent is he who mounts'; Aeschylus *The Eumenides* tr Richard Latimore (New York 1967) lines 658–60.
23 'Economic and Philosophical Manuscripts' 139
24 Ibid
25 Marx and Engels *German Ideology* ed Pascal 17–18
26 *Capital* I pt I ch I sec 4
27 Ibid 89–90
28 'Economic and Philosophical Manuscripts' 105

Nietzsche's Ambivalence about Women

CHRISTINE GARSIDE ALLEN

Ambivalence is one of the most common and most difficult human qualities to live with. It has a peculiar form which seems to defy the law of non-contradiction. It can be both emotional and intellectual in content and can be directed towards the self, towards others, and towards events and social change. Nietzsche stands as a man who gave evidence of ambivalence towards many different things: towards Germans, Christ, Jews, saints, disciples, philosophers, and women. Jaspers ironically turns this quality into a virtue when he states that in order to understand Nietzsche's view on any subject it is necessary to take one statement on the subject and then search for its opposite.[1] However, ambivalence has its negative side both for the person living it and for those upon whom it is projected. It is the sign of an unintegrated person. Lack of integration is not always detrimental, for it often is a sign of growth. If someone is leaving an old pattern of life for a new one, ambivalence would be a natural accompaniment. Sometimes, however, ambivalence seems to give no evidence of growth, but rather of a static personality trapped in conflicting hopes, desires, and ideas. Nietzsche's ambivalence towards women appears to be an example of this static ambivalence.

Today, as a result of the changes which women's liberation is bringing for women and men, there is a great deal of ambivalence connected with the question of woman's identity and man's identity. The ambivalence of growth which women feel between their femininity and their humanity was first recognized by de Beauvoir and more recently documented by Bardwick.[2] Very little has been done to document the ambivalence that men feel. A close study of Nietzsche offers an opportunity to begin this work. Nietzsche can serve as a magnifying mirror for the ambivalence of contemporary men because his ideas, which are stated in extremes, allow us to pinpoint the foci of the ambivalence. As will be seen, these foci are the same, for the most part, as those which appear time and again in discussions about women's liberation. A study of Nietzsche's ambivalence about women can be of value to men today who are trying to uncover the roots of their own ambivalence. It can be of equal value to women who by working through their own reactions to a philosopher as articulate as Nietzsche can become better able to cope with the more subtle ambivalence which they encounter in everyday situations. Finally, it is a study which has the goal of knowledge for its own sake. To this date a comprehensive account of Nietzsche's views on women has not been published.

The first form ambivalence takes in Nietzsche's theory is his double claim that women are weak and strong. Woman's weakness can be seen in terms of her relationship to slave morality, and her strength by her closeness to the Dionysian element in life. We find Nietzsche claiming: 'Finally: woman! One-half of mankind is weak, typically sick, changeable, inconstant – woman needs strength in order to cleave to it; she needs a religion that glorifies being weak, loving, and being humble as divine.' Weakness or impotence of power tends to create a morality to justify itself rather than seek to change the balance of power. Nietzsche often uses this characteristic of women as an adjective to describe *any* weak or decadent group. 'What is womanish, what stems from slavishness and especially from the mob hopscotch: *that* now wants to become master of mankind's entire destiny – oh disgust! disgust!' disgust!'[3]

A further characteristic of this weakness is the inability to be perceptive about the self. Nietzsche describes this as a 'deliberate closing of one's eyes to oneself,' as a lack of 'psychological cleanliness,' and as a lack of depth. While he sometimes hints that women are this way because innocence is attractive to men, more often he argues that it is her nature to be so. '(Women) believe in the superficiality of existence as in its essence.' Her nature is a surface, whereas man's is deep. The quality of self perception is crucial to Nietzsche's thought and constitutes one of the necessary characteristics for all self-overcoming. However, he claims 'Women are so constituted that all truth ... disgusts them.'[4]

The word 'feminism' characterizes this negative female quality: 'All "Feminism," too – also in men – closes the door; it will never permit entrance into this labyrinth of audacious insights. One must never have spared oneself, one must have acquired hardness as a habit to be cheerful and in good spirits in the midst of nothing but hard truths.'[5] Finally, the adjective 'feminine' is used to condemn a kind of weak nobility, pernicious feelings, feeble dissatisfaction, a shallow spirit, and the romanticism of the eighteenth and nineteenth centuries. In Nietzsche's characterization of woman's weakness we find the traditional litany of negative feminine qualities.

In contrast to this negative projection of woman's identity we find Nietzsche often expressing an opposite point of view. 'What inspires respect for woman, and often enough even fear, is her *nature* which is more "natural" than man's, the genuine, cunning suppleness of a beast of prey, the tiger's claw under the glove, the naïveté of her egoism, her ineducability and inner wildness, the incomprehensibility, scope, and movement of her desires and virtues.'[6] Woman's nature is like that of Dionysus, the Greek god Nietzsche turns to for a model of rebirth for European man. He is a god of ecstasy, joy, affirmation, and the will to life. In *Thus Spake Zarathustra* young girls symbolize joy and lightheartedness, a necessary antidote to the spirit of gravity.

This symbolism is inverted when Nietzsche refers to the ecstacy of *nature* crying out through Dionysian art: 'I am the eternally creative primordial mother, eternally impelling to existence.'[7] Dionysian art calls the philosopher back into the *womb* of the true reality and the *bosom* of the Primordial one. Music, the natural home for the Dionysian spirit, also is described as the *motherly* womb in contrast to the plastic arts which more clearly represent Apollo.[8] Here woman is projected as strong, as a source for new life in contrast to the images mentioned above where she is identified with the morality of the weak. It is true to Nietzsche's style not to make distinctions between some women who are weak and some who are strong. In most cases he refers either to women as a group or to female symbols. The one exception is when he singles out feminists who seek equal rights. This group of women is given a different sort of critique as we shall see later.

Women of the status quo then are both weak and strong at the same time. Nietzsche hates what he considers to be their weakness and is fascinated by what he considers to be their strength. This fascination leads him to advocate the use of force to maintain the status quo. The old woman tells Zarathustra: 'Are you visiting women? Do not forget your whip.'[9] Nietzsche hopes by the use of force to preserve the strength of the Dionysian element in life. Paradoxically, however, the result of this use of force would be to produce women who are *both* strong *and* weak.

In *Beyond Good and Evil* Nietzsche draws out more clearly the kind of forced domination he advocates. Woman must be 'repressed,' 'kept under control,' 'locked up lest it fly away,' 'possessed,' 'predestined for service,' and 'kept afraid of man.'[10] The paradox is that precisely this action of man towards woman would result in developing the negative character traits of slave morality which Nietzsche claimed was spreading over Europe. His ambivalence about women led him to make a claim for the value of forced repression of women to enhance the presence of the Dionysian element in life without allowing him to foresee the consequences of this action for the omnipresence of slave morality.

This ambivalence is seen to have even greater consequences when one considers Nietzsche's desire to create the conditions within which the possibility for a higher type of human life would exist. One of the central tasks of the superman is to become free from the desire for revenge. When a person is repressed the obvious correlate of this repression is the desire for revenge. Nietzsche recognizes this when he considers the other side of slave morality to be a hidden tyrant. 'Woman is vengeful: that is due to her weakness, as much as is her susceptibility to the distress of others.' And yet he insists that marriage be established on the basis of the 'drive to dominate.' Women must be kept afraid of men. She must 'unconditionally submit' and he must 'take possession.'[11]

This forced repression of women, and its consequences – perpetuation of slave morality and the desire for revenge – lead us into Nietzsche's second fundamental ambivalence towards women. This ambivalence is centred in Nietzsche's own identity as a man and the relation of that to the ability to give birth. He wanted to maintain that women were fundamentally *biological* parents, that through them Dionysian forces would be transmitted, and that if women were not dominated they would lose this energy. He did not consider the *psychological* or spiritual dimension of child-rearing by the mother to be significant. It is the male artists who will deliver the higher men from revenge and pave the way for the superman.

Nietzsche's writing abounds with maternal metaphors. In *Thus Spake Zarathustra* he states: 'for the creator himself to be the child new-born he must also be willing to be the mother and endure the mother's pain.' In *Ecce Homo* he compares himself as a philosopher to a pregnant woman. 'Has it been noted that in that profound tension to which pregnancy condemns the spirit, and at bottom the whole organism, chance and any kind of stimulus from the outside have too vehement an effect and strike too deep. One must avoid chance and outside stimuli as much as possible; a kind of walling oneself in belongs among the foremost instinctive precautions of spiritual pregnancy.' Nietzsche also uses such expressions as 'unconscious pregnancy of destined individuals,' 'supplemental pregnancy of those who arrive at works and deeds,' 'sterility of gifted minds who are too impatient to wait for their pregnancy', and intellectual pregnancy of contemplatives who are the 'masculine mothers.' The philosopher is impregnated by ideas, protects himself from intrusion during the time of gestation, waits for the natural term of gestation to be over, and gives birth in pain. He is, as Nietzsche so poignantly said, a 'masculine mother.'[12]

Is it surprising that Nietzsche would feel ambivalent about the motherhood of women unless it could be clearly delineated from the motherhood of men? The closeness between Nietzsche's identity and woman's identity is even more evident when we consider the function of the Dionysian element once again. Nietzsche claims that he is able to understand women better because of his similarity to them. 'May I here venture the surmise that I *know* women? That is part of my Dionysian dowry. Who knows? Perhaps I am the first psychologist of the eternally feminine?'[13] Nietzsche's identification with Dionysus was given its ultimate expression in a letter to Cosima Wagner after his mental breakdown in 1889. The letter stated simply: 'Ariadne, I love you' and was signed 'Dionysus.'[14] Nietzsche's ambivalence was then related to his having identified women as the protector of the Dionysian element in life, and yet having found himself much closer to the Dionysian forces than to the Apollonian.

Nietzsche tried to solve this ambivalence by reducing women's function to the biological level of procreation by developing a two-level concept of the Dionysian, and by excluding women from the higher level of Dionysian life. In *Thus Spake Zarathustra* women are told 'Let your hope be: "May I bear the Superman."' He admires Greek civilization where 'women had no other mission than to produce beautiful, strong bodies, in which the father's character lived on as unbrokenly as possible.' He wants women to concentrate on the preparation of good food for human development. Finally, he worries about modern German music making women 'more incapable of her first and last profession – to give birth to strong children.'[15] If Nietzsche can separate out the functions of women and men so that women are biological mothers and men spiritual mothers then there is no need to fear the closeness of their identity.

Furthermore, he is able to solidify this polarity by distinguishing two groups of men: those who procreate and those who do not. Reflecting the view commonly held in the nineteenth century that the energy of men is depleted by love-making, Nietzsche claims: 'As for the "chastity" of philosophers, finally this type of spirit clearly has its fruitfulness somewhere else than in children ... Every artist knows what a harmful effect intercourse has in states of great spiritual tension and preparation.' The higher men then have no biological function in parenting the superman; their function is spiritual. The 'masculine mothers' appear to be mothers of the spirit, not the flesh. And yet, this polarity between spirit and flesh seems to be just the polarity that Nietzsche is attempting to destroy when he claims that: 'The awakened, the enlightened man says: I am body entirely, and nothing beside; the soul is only a word for something in the body.'[16] Nietzsche's ambivalence then has to remain for it is clear that women and men cannot be distinguished in such a simple duality.

Nietzsche's development of a two-level notion of the Dionysian follows the same pattern. In the first case the Dionysian represents the crude energies which seem to characterize women's wildness, naturalness, lightheartedness, and joy. As Sandra Frisby has expressed it, 'Nietzsche sees the role of woman as being clearly that of preserving the Dionysian element, the element of unrefined passion. He suggests that this role is of a preconscious nature; that woman is formed of passions, of instincts, of sensual response as though she had received these from some primordial font, and was now their guardian, the fortress of their preservation.'[17]

The first level of Dionysian force is undeveloped, or childlike. The second level, however, appears to be a new innocence which has incorporated the Apollonian dynamic. The third stage of evolution in *Thus Spake Zarathustra*, the child, gives evidence of a new innocence, a 'yea saying, a new joy.' Women have the first level of Dionysian force, but not the second. Most men have the Apollonian element. A few artist-philosophers have both, but not yet in integration, and a small number of these few have been able to pass into a higher stage of development to a new level of Dionysian life or refinement of the will to power, where the two elements are integrated into a higher Dionysian force.

The exclusion of women from the artistic process is made clear by the language of Nietzsche's writings. 'The intricate relation of the Apollonian and the Dionysian in tragedy may really be symbolized by a *fraternal union* of the two Deities: Dionysus speaks the language of Apollo; and Apollo, finally the language of Dionysus; and so the highest goal of tragedy and of all art is attained.'[18] Male force coupled with male force gives birth to the tragic spirit. The exclusion of women is also seen by the absence of any women in Zarathustra's cave.[19] Finally it is made evident by the strong attacks Nietzsche makes on the feminists who, through their attempt to gain access to education and to the political world, threatened to overturn the delicate balance between Apollo and Dionysus which Nietzsche believed to be so central to life.

The third ambivalence in Nietzsche to be considered in this paper concerns his personal attraction to women of intellect and culture and his simultaneous belief that education destroys woman's Dionysian instincts. In *Twilight of the Idols* Nietzsche asks: 'What is the task of all higher education? – to turn man into a machine?' Classical education with its emphasis on memory and culture draws the mind outward into imitation instead of inward into self-knowledge and the creation of new values. The desire of women to have education becomes then a desire to imitate the 'stupidities' of men. It focuses on the order, harmony, and seriousness of the Apollonian instead of the chaos, wildness, and light-hearted joy of the Dionysian. 'The emancipation of woman ... is thus seen to be an odd symptom of the increasing weakening and dulling of the most feminine instincts.' Again and again Nietzsche laments that woman is 'losing the ground on which she is most certain of victory,' 'neglecting practice with her proper weapons,' 'loosing her instincts,' and having her instincts 'crumble.'[20]

He approaches this same problem from another angle by arguing that women's strength comes from the preservation of her instincts and will. 'The most powerful and influential women of the world ... owed their power and ascendency over men to the force of their will ... and not to their schoolmasters.' Furthermore, because Nietzsche is so concerned to regain the balance of the Dionysian element, he considers it as higher in rank than the Apollonian and woman by virtue of her closeness to it has higher rank than the average Apollonian man. In *Ecce Homo* he states: 'Woman, *the more she is a woman*, resists rights in general hand and foot: after all, the state of nature, the eternal war between the sexes gives her by far the first rank.'[21]

Some aspects of these two approaches to feminism might well receive the approbation of some feminists today. Education often seems to destroy something instinctive in women. While this claim is true for men as well, there is a certain further dynamic to the educational system which is only now coming under careful study by feminists, namely that women feel alienated from a great deal that is taught because they are invisible within it. This of course is not a condemnation of education per se but merely of education as it has developed within western patriarchal society. Another aspect of the above approach which some feminists might enjoy is Nietzsche's claim that women are naturally first-rank. The claim that women are so much better than men has been echoed down the centuries. John Stuart Mill, in his classic feminist work, *On the Subjection of Women*, gave the wonderful rejoinder to this claim: If women are so much better then why must they be put under the control of men?[22] When Nietzsche talks about higher rank, he only means that they begin from a better place, not that they end first. As shown previously, women are excluded from the higher ranks of existence.

Nietzsche was determined to keep the emancipation of women from occurring, and he began a third approach to feminism to complement the above two approaches, which lament the loss of instincts and exhort women to stay in their natural place of 'first rank.' This third approach consisted in launching attacks on the identity of feminists with the fundamental claim that they were not women. In the above quotation from *Ecce Homo* we saw a subtle phrase which indicates this approach: 'Woman, *the more she is a woman*, resists rights hand and foot.' This claim however, is made even more explicit: 'Emancipation of woman – that is the instinctive hatred of the abortive woman, who is incapable of giving birth, against the woman who is turned out well.'[23] Women who chose emancipation are *incapable* of giving birth.

This view of Nietzsche's is in stark contrast to his view of artistic men who *chose* not to give birth so that they might use their energies for spiritual creation. Furthermore, he implies that women's liberation is based on a desire for revenge against women who are biological mothers. Nietzsche's lack of insight here is glaring. He recognizes the conflict 'aut liberi aut libri' (either children or books).' that faces women who consider choosing a path other than biological motherhood. However, Nietzsche does not give an acceptable analysis of the reasons for this conflict. Women have had to choose children or books because of the plain fact that to do both jobs involves extraordinary energy. As Lorenne Clarke and Lynda Lange have pointed out, reproduction has not yet been democratized.[24]

Nietzsche's implication that women who seek education are not really women is clearly expressed in *Beyond Good and Evil*. 'When a woman has scholarly inclinations there is usually something wrong with her sexuality.'[25] This view is not new to philosophy. Kant had claimed that women who wanted to learn Greek might as well grow a beard, Kierkegaard had called women who sought to develop their reflective powers 'unwomanly,' and Freud accused women who dared to succeed in a man's world of being castrating and driven by penis envy. In effect Nietzsche is charging women who seek emancipation with sterility. Since he had so closely defined woman's identity with the biological function of motherhood, it follows that emancipated women are not really women. Furthermore, he draws the logical consequences of this when he claims: 'Everything about woman is a riddle, and everything about woman has one solution. It is called pregnancy.'[26] In order to keep the division of the sexes clear, women must be contained within the role of biological motherhood. While this approach may have brought Nietzsche some relief from the danger of role-confusion in his calling to be a masculine mother, it clearly did not persuade the feminists.

Nietzsche's ambivalence about educated women is seen even more clearly in the circumstances of his personal life. The two women whom he loved were both independent and liberated by the standards of the nineteenth century. Cosima Wagner, the illegitimate daughter of Franz Liszt and mistress, later wife, of Richard Wagner, was a woman of great learning. Nietzsche was devoted to her as an older woman while he was a young man. This devotion did not abate even though his affection for Richard Wagner changed dramatically. In *Ecce Homo*, written near the end of his life, Nietzsche refers to Cosima Wagner as 'by far the first voice in taste I have ever heard.'[27] Lou Andréas-Salomé was younger than Nietzsche. Soon after he had met her he felt he had found a disciple to carry on his work. In a letter he wrote to her: 'Back in Orta I conceived the plan of leading you step by step to the final consequences of my philosophy – *you* as the first person I took to be fit for this.' He wrote about her to Franz Overbeck, to his sister, to Peter Gast, and to Malwide von Meysenburg.[28] In all of this correspondence the same theme was repeated over and over. He had found someone to carry on his ideas.

This high hope which Nietzsche had placed in Lou Salomé did not bear the expected fruit. She had her own ideas and did not want to become Nietzsche's blueprint. As Rudolph Binion describes it in *Frau Lou* 'Lou called on Nietzsche to clarify his intentions toward her, which ... she now took to be secretarial use and sexual abuse.' Nietzsche tried to set things right in a letter (26 June) 'Never did I think that you should "read aloud and write" for me, but I very much wished that I might be your *teacher*. To tell the whole truth: I am now seeking people who could be my heirs.'[29] However, Paul Rée, who also desired Lou's attention, continued to distort Nietzsche's intentions towards her. In addition, pressures were exerted on Nietzsche by his sister and mother to break

this relationship because of Lou Salomé's 'liberated' life-style of tra-
velling and living freely with men, however chaste the relationships
might have been. These pressures would not have been enough had
Nietzsche not discovered that Lou and Paul Rée had been speaking
about him in a destructive way to others. Ten months after they met, he
terminated the relationship permanently.

It is important here to recognize the profound effect that Lou Salomé
had on Nietzsche's development and perhaps the equally strong effect
she had by the break in the relationship. Who knows what different
directions Nietzsche's thought might have taken if he and Lou Salomé
had been able to form a long-lasting and deep relationship? John Stuart
Mill claimed he learned most of what he knew about women from
Harriet Taylor; Karl Jaspers described his wife's major contribution to
his experience of philosophy as a 'loving struggle.'

I believe Nietzsche would have developed differently if he had been
able to sustain a dialogue with Lou Salomé. His writing about women
before and during their relationship opens the door to new possibilities
in woman's identity; immediately after the break the door is slammed
shut. In the late 1870s Nietzsche wrote *Human All Too Human* in which
he devoted an entire section to the subject 'Wife and Child.' He seemed
to be thinking of marriage at this point and had made a written proposal
to a young girl, Mathilde Trampedaor.[30] There appears to have been little
personal contact between the two and he was not affected much by the
immediate refusal. In *Human All Too Human* we find the interesting claim
that 'the perfect woman is a higher type of humanity than the perfect
man, and also something much rarer.'[31] He was probably reflecting his
admiration for Cosima Wagner, but the possibility for full human development of woman is here.

He met Lou Salomé in the spring of 1882 and during this year he
published *Joyful Wisdom*. This book says little about women but what it
says is extremely innovative: 'A powerful contralto voice, as we occa-
sionally hear it in the theatre, raises suddenly for us the curtain *on possibilities in which we usually do not believe*; all at once we are convinced that
somewhere in the world there may be women with high, heroic, royal
souls, capable and prepared for magnificent remonstrances, resolutions,
and self-sacrifices, capable and prepared for domination over men, because in them the best in man, superior to sex has become a corporeal
ideal.'[32] In this extraordinary passage we find Nietzsche raising the curtain on 'possibilities in which we do not usually believe.' He is clearly

excited by these possibilities, open to them, and willing to consider women as capable of the fullest philosophical development.

Then Lou's 'betrayal,' among other things, brought this curtain crashing down, and Nietzsche never again considers women in the same way. By December 1882 he decided to live alone 'as a hermit'; and in January the first book of *Thus Spake Zarathustra* was written.[33] In this work nearly all the direct statements about women are negative. They are shallow and slavish; they should be dominated by a whip; and the solution to their problems is pregnancy. Only in symbolic form does he allow any positive feelings for women to emerge. He would marry Eternity; Life is a great woman; and the stillest hour is his mistress.[34]

Clearly a profound change occurred in Nietzsche's thinking at this point. He stopped considering the potentiality for growth in real women and has returned to the traditional intellectual split between the abstract idealized Eternal Feminine in all its positive qualities and the Eternal Feminine in all its negative qualities. He only individualizes women again when he turns to attack the feminists. The infamous passages from *Beyond Good and Evil*, which are in part a parody of some aphorisms Lou had written earlier, demonstrate this point adequately.[35] 'Woman wants to become self-reliant – and for that reason she is beginning to enlighten men about "woman as such": *this* is one of the worst developments of the general *uglification* of Europe.'[36]

Lou Salomé did not cease her efforts to write about women or to lead an independent life. She was a well-known literary critic, philosopher, and psychoanalytic biographer. She formed relationships of differing degrees with Rilke, Ibsen, and Freud. Again it is worth thinking about the possible effect she could have had on Nietzsche had circumstances been different. When she met him she was very young and extremely puritanical. After her marriage to Fred Charles Andréas she seemed to open up sexually and later moved easily into affairs. It seems probable that Nietzsche wanted a sexual relationship with her and that she rejected his advances rather brutally. She was an extremely straight forward person and probably brought a great deal of intensity into a personal relationship.

It is precisely her sort of insight which can bring about tremendous personal growth in marriage. A short passage from the book she wrote on Nietzsche indicates one such insight into his personality. '"Il existe deux espèces de génies", dit-il un jour, "ceux qui veulent avant tout *créer*, et qui créent; et ceux qui aiment à se laisser féconder, et qui *enfantent*. Il est certain qu'il appartenait à cette seconde catégorie. Il y avait dans son tempérament quelque chose de féminin, mais porté à un degré de grandeur incomparable!"'[37] Lou's recognition of Nietzsche's femininity and simultaneous affirmation of its 'incomparable grandeur' would have gone far to alleviate his own ambivalence about this quality in himself if it had been reflected in a long-term loving relationship. Unfortunately, Nietzsche was too ill by the time this book was published to benefit from any of Lou's insights.

The fourth and final ambivalence in Nietzsche's views about women must really be seen in the broader context of his basic philosophy and love of conflict. He believed that it was only through struggle that growth occurred. One's best friend was one's enemy; aphorisms were written in blood; and truths were discovered by leaping from mountain top to mountain top. Even the higher men were chastised, not encouraged, and left alone in the cave with a cry of distress.[38] The intensity and excitement generated by Nietzsche's proclamations gained a great deal of their color by his extremism towards others. Indeed Nietzsche's reflections about his teacher demonstrate a remarkable similarity between the two philosophers. 'We should not underestimate the fact that Schopenhauer, who treated sexuality as a personal enemy (including its tool woman that "instrumentum diaboli") *needed* enemies in order to keep in good spirits ... Without these Schopenhauer would *not* have persisted.' Nietzsche's own delight in attacking his enemies reflects his basic claim that 'every growth is indicated by the search for a mighty opponent or problem.'[39] Women were just one such opponent or problem.

The ambivalence Nietzsche felt towards women, then, was part of a general ambivalence he felt towards anything he loved and hated at the same time. He evidenced the same complex range of emotions towards Germans, Jews, Christ, saints, philosophers, and others. However, in the case of woman, he linked this ambivalence to a view of the necessary polarity of the sexes. 'The continuous development of art is bound up with the Apollonian and Dionysian duality – just as procreation depends on the duality of the sexes, involving perpetual strife with only periodic intervening reconciliations.' Nietzsche expresses this theme of 'perpetual strife' between the sexes in many different ways: 'Love – in its means, war; at bottom, the deadly hatred of the sexes.'[40]

In order to increase the tensions of energy and will-to-power in the world Nietzsche insists upon a polarity of strife. Even when he speaks in feminine metaphors, the same theme occurs. 'From the heart of me I love only Life and in truth, I love her most of all when I hate her!'[41] This duality of the sexes which I call 'false sex-polarity' is based upon the false assumption that women and men have certain natural qualities which are uniquely theirs by virtue of being born female or male. For Nietzsche these qualities are those most closely associated with Dionysus, e.g. joy, spontaneity, lightness, wildness, and so on. Men are similarly supposed to be given 'natural' propensities for reflection, seriousness, capacities for individuation, and so on. That this false polarity is the result of socialization has now been generally recognized.

In addition to the basic assumption of a false sex-polarity, Nietzsche makes the further mistaken judgment that education will inevitably turn women into men. 'To go wrong on the fundamental problem of "man and woman" to deny the most abysmal antagonism between them and the necessity of eternally hostile tension, to dream perhaps of equal rights, equal education, equal claims and obligations – that is a *typical* sign of shallowness.' It is clear that to Nietzsche woman's access to public life will destroy the natural antagonism between the sexes which he believes is necessary for procreation and for growth in general. His delight in an all-out war against the rising feminism of the nineteenth century is most evident in a letter he wrote to his sister Elizabeth in 1885: 'All those who rave about "the emancipation of women" have slowly, ever so slowly, come to realize that I am their "bad animal." In Zurich the women students burst into a great rage against me. Finally! – and *how* many of these "at lasts" do I have to look forward to?!'[42]

Nietzsche's fear that emancipated women will become just like men has been felt by many people. Indeed some of the strongest feminists have made this their goal. However, I believe that emancipation of women will result in a true sex-polarity in which women and men become who they are. In another paper I have developed this theme in detail.[43]

Briefly, true sex-polarity claims that women and men are born with similar capacities to experience life. This means that they have equal access to what Nietzsche describes as the Dionysian and Apollonian elements, however much they may differ in the content of their life-experience through the differences they receive by virtue of being female or male. Specifically they differ in their recent past, their inherited past, their present context, their body, their relation to language, and therefore to their possibilities in the future. There will always be a polarity between women and men. This polarity will be significant in some contexts and not in others.

In summary, this essay has examined four different kinds of ambivalence in Nietzsche's theory of women. The first ambivalence was seen to be aimed towards women of the status quo. Nietzsche admired the Dionysian aspect of woman while detesting her weakness and tendency towards 'slave morality.' His admiration, however, led him to advocate forced repression of women in marriage. He did not seem to be aware of the paradox that this forced repression would perpetuate the characteristics of slave morality as well.

The second ambivalence resulted from Nietzsche's definition of woman's identity as particularly close to the Dionysian element in life and in the function of giving birth, while at the same time recognizing that his own nature was more like women than like men in these two respects. He tried to solve this ambivalence by dividing motherhood into the biological and spiritual categories. However, this went against his more basic view that the body and spirit are one.

The third ambivalence was derived from his personal attraction to women of intellect, culture, and will, and his simultaneous fear that woman's emancipation will destroy women's instincts. We saw that this fear was based on the false supposition that if women enter into education and public life they will become like men. On the contrary, I claim that the release of women into public life will result in the eventual development of a true sex-polarity.

The final ambivalence seen in Nietzsche's theory of women was the general ambivalence he felt towards loving what he hates, having his enemies for friends, seeking opponents for growth. He believed that women and men have to be in perpetual strife within this broader context.

At the outset it was claimed that Nietzsche's ambivalence towards women was an example of static ambivalence. This kind of ambivalence was contrasted with an ambivalence of growth or change. Ambivalence in itself is not necessarily a bad quality. Nietzsche himself was aware of its natural presence when 'old tables' are being destroyed to make way for new values. In fact, one of the most powerful dynamics of Nietzsche's writings comes from his insight into the tendency within human beings to cling to the old for security, even when it has ceased to be useful or creative. Those who are breaking new ground must learn to live with this sort of ambivalence. In addition, if they wish to live with joy, they must enter into the ambivalence with an acceptance and *amor fati* which would allow them the will to enter the same life (even to re-enter it under the theory of the 'eternal return'). Nietzsche's insights here would be helpful both to feminists who are creating new values for woman's identity and for those men who are genuinely trying to live out the consequences of these new values in their lives.

Nietzsche's theory of woman, however, does not give any evidence of being on the same level of sophistication as many of his other theories. The ambivalence he shows towards women is not due to any growth or breaking of old tables. It is static from beginning to end. The only exception is a short interim period of one or two years during his relationship with Lou Salomé when he seemed to open the possibility for growth, but then closed it. The conclusive evidence for the static quality of Nietzsche's theory of woman is found in a careful comparison of the entire corpus of his works.

The method used in this paper was to take each remark Nietzsche made about women, to consider it within the context of the book within which it is found, to compare it with remarks in other books, to compare it with his personal correspondence of the same period, and to consider the opinions of others towards his life. The result was the discovery that Nietzsche held the same views about women at the beginning of his life as at the end, and that these remarks did not show any discrepancy within any of the works he had written. In each case the same general characteristics of women were found.

What then of static ambivalence? Is it possible for a Nietzschean to evade this condemnation by appealing once more to *amor fati*? If we are to become who we are, and we find ourselves locked in static ambivalence, should we try to will it, love our fate, and rejoice in saying 'yea'? I do not think so. Static ambivalence is destructive for those on whom it is projected. In this case, it is destructive for women of the status quo every bit as much as for feminists.

Being the recipient of 'double messages' takes a great deal of energy which might much more productively be placed elsewhere. Furthermore, it is painful for the person projecting it. The lack of integration which it shows also takes energy to protect, to hold together, and to live out. This energy could be better used in self-overcoming. Nietzsche held as an ultimate ideal the wholesome integration of the superman whose only ambivalence and suffering came from continual growth and creation of new values. Static ambivalence, then, is contrary to the ideal of the superman. It will take woman's energy to recognize and criticize such static ambivalence, and it will take man's energy to begin to assimilate this information and embrace it as a catalyst for his own growth. Mutually we can go forward in this lifelong process of self-overcoming.

REFERENCES

1 Karl Jaspers *Nietzsche* tr C. Wallraff and F. Schmitz (Chicago 1966) 10
2 De Beauvoir *The Second Sex* (New York 1974) 796–814; Judith Bardwick and Elizabeth Douvan 'Ambivalence: The Socialization of Woman' in V. Gornick and B. Moran eds *Woman in Sexist Society* (New York 1971) 225–41
3 *The Will to Power* tr W. Kaufman and R.J. Hollingdale (New York 1968) 460 #864 (1888); *Thus Spoke Zarathustra* tr R.J. Hollingdale (Harmondsworth 1969) 298
4 *Will to Power* 245 #806 (1883–8); *Ecce Homo and The Genealogy of Morals* tr W. Kaufman (New York 1967) 322; *Joyful Wisdom* tr T. Common (New York 1973) 101 #64; *Zarathustra* 92; *Human All Too Human* tr P.V. Cohn in O. Levy ed *The Complete Works of Friedrich Nietzsche* VII (Edinburgh 1911) pt 1, 140 #286
5 *Ecce Homo* 264 #3
6 *Beyond Good and Evil* tr W. Kaufman (New York 1966) 169
7 *The Birth of Tragedy* tr W. Kaufman (New York 1967) 109
8 Ibid 2, 65, 126, 131
9 *Zarathustra* 93
10 *Beyond Good and Evil* 163, 166, 168
11 *Ecce Homo* 232; *Will to Power* 388 #732 (1888)
12 *Zarathustra* 111; *Ecce Homo* 242; *Human* I 10–11, II 40 #63, II 110 #216; *Joyful Wisdom* 105 #72; Rudolph Binion *Frau Lou* (Princeton 1968) 102–3, letter to Hans von Bulow (1882)
13 *Ecce Homo* 266
14 *Selected Letters of Friedrich Nietzsche* tr and ed C. Middleton (Chicago 1969) 346, letter #204 to Cosima Wagner
15 *Zarathustra* 92; *Human* 238 #259; *Beyond Good and Evil* 164 #234, 169 #239
16 *Genealogy of Morals* 107, 111, 117; *Zarathustra* 61
17 Sandra Frisby 'Women and the Will to Power' *Gnosis* I 2 (1975) 2
18 *Birth of Tragedy* 130, 132
19 *Zarathustra* 289–90
20 *Beyond Good and Evil* 168–9; *Human* I 311 #425; *Will to Power* 433 #817 (1888)
21 *Beyond Good and Evil* 168; *Ecce Homo* 267
22 John Stuart Mill *The Subjection of Women* (Cambridge, Mass. 1972) 76
23 *Ecce Homo* 266, 267

24 Lorenne Clark 'The Rights of Women' in J. King-Farlow and W. Shea eds
   Contemporary Issues in Political Philosophy (New York 1976) 49–65; Lynda
   Lange 'Reproduction in Democratic Theory' in ibid 131–46
25 *Beyond Good and Evil* 89 #144
26 *Zarathustra* 93
27 *Ecce Homo* 243
28 Binion *Frau Lou* 52, 68, 69; K. Leidecker *Nietzsche Unpublished Letters*
   (New York 1959) 86, 89, 209
29 Binion *Frau Lou* 67
30 Leidecker *Unpublished Letters* 67
31 *Human* 294 #377
32 *Joyful Wisdom* 103 #70
33 Binion *Frau Lou* 101–2
34 *Zarathustra* 83, 91–3, 132, 167, 241, 244–7
35 Binion *Frau Lou* 129
36 *Beyond Good and Evil* 162 #232
37 Lou Andréas-Salomé *Friedrich Nietzsche* tr Jacques Benoit-Méchin
   (Paris 1970) 55
38 *Zarathustra* 296–306
39 *Genealogy of Morals* 106 #7; *Ecce Homo* 232
40 *Birth of Tragedy* 33; *Ecce Homo* 267
41 *Zarathustra* 132
42 *Beyond Good and Evil* 405 #637; Leidecker *Unpublished Letters* 114
43 Christine Garside Allen 'Sex Identity and Personal Identity' in J. King-
   Farlow and W. Shea eds *Values and the Quality of Life* (New York 1976)
   93–126

Bibliography

The following bibliography lists recent feminist work on the subjects of the essays contained in this anthology. There is also a bibliography for general topics of importance to political feminism. We have included some of the unpublished works in this rapidly developing field, with the departments and universities of the respective authors from whom copies may be requested. The categories are inevitably somewhat arbitrary.

Any omission of recent feminist work on these subjects, published or unpublished, is probably an oversight, and should not be taken to indicate the authors' disagreement or judgment of its worth.

MAJOR PHILOSOPHERS

Alexander, W.M. 'Philosophers Have Avoided Sex' *Diogenes* LXXII (1970) 56–74
Allen, Christine Garside 'Plato on Women' *Feminist Studies* II 2–3 (1975) 131–8
Annas, Julia 'Mill and the Subjection of Women' *Philosophy* LII (1977) 179–94
– 'Plato's *Republic* and Feminism' *Philosophy* LI (1976) 307–21
Anon, N. 'Did Nietzsche Predict the Superwoman as Well as the Superman?' *Current Literature* XLIII (1907) 633–4
Burns, Steven A.M. 'The Humean Female' *Dialogue* XIV (1976) 415–24
– 'The Platonic Women: Philosophy as a Subversive Activity' unpublished, Dept. of Philosophy, Dalhousie University
Calvert, Brian 'Plato and the Equality of Women' *Phoenix* XXIX (1975) 231–43
Collins, Margery, and Pierce, Christine 'Holes and Slime: Sexism in Sartre's Psychoanalysis' in C.C. Gould and M. Wartofsky eds *Women and Philosophy: Toward a Theory of Liberation* New York 1976
Fortenbaugh, W.W. 'On Plato's Feminism in *Republic* V' *Apeiron* IX (1975) 1–4

Frisby, Sandra 'Women and the Will to Power' *Gnosis* I 2 (1975) 1–10

Horowitz, Maryanne Cline 'Aristotle and Women' *Journal of the History of Biology* IX (1976) 183–213

Keohane, Nannerl O. '"But For Her Sex ...": the Domestication of Sophie' *Trent Rousseau Papers* in *University of Ottawa Review* forthcoming and *Collection Philosophica* forthcoming

Lange, Lynda 'Woman is Not a Rational Animal: On Aristotle's Biology of Reproduction' unpublished, Dept. of Philosophy, University of Toronto

Marcil-Lacoste, Louise 'The Consistency of Hume's Position Concerning Women' *Dialogue* XIV (1976) 425–40

– 'Les coefficients idéologiques de l'appel sentiments chez Rousseau' Proceedings of the International Colloquium on Jean-Jacques Rousseau et la société du XVIIIème siècle, McGill University, Montreal, October 1978, forthcoming

O'Brien, Mary 'Hegel: Man, Physiology and Fate?' unpublished, Dept. of Sociology, Ontario Institute for Studies in Education, Toronto

Okin, Susan Moller 'Philosopher Queens and Private Wives: Plato on Women and the Family' *Philosophy and Public Affairs* VI 4 (1977) 345–69

– 'Rousseau's Natural Women' *Journal of Politics* XLI 2 (1979) 393–416

Parsons, Kathryn Pine 'Nietzsche and Moral Change' in R. Solomon ed *Nietzsche: A Collection of Critical Essays* New York 1973

Pierce, Christine 'Equality: *Republic* V' *Monist* LVII (1973) 1–11

Pomeroy, Sarah B. 'Feminism in Book V of Plato's *Republic*' *Apeiron* VIII (May 1974) 32–4

Saxonhouse, Arlene W. 'The Philosopher and Woman in the Political Thought of Plato' *Political Theory* IV (1976) 195–212

Silver, Marie-France 'Jean-Jacques Rousseau and the Position of Women in 18th Century French Society' unpublished, Dept. of French and Hispanic Studies, York University, Toronto

MARXISM

Benston, Margaret 'The Political Economy of Women's Liberation' *Monthly Review* XXI 4 (1969) 13–27

Clark, Lorenne M.G. 'A Marxist-Feminist Critique of Marx and Engels; or, The Consequences of Seizing the Reins in the Household' unpublished, Dept. of Philosophy, University of Toronto

Delphy, Christine 'The Main Enemy: A Materialist Analysis of Women's Repression' tr from *Partisans* special issue 'Libération des femmes' Paris 1970

Dixon, Marlene 'Women's Liberation: Opening Chapter Two' *Canadian Dimension* x 8 (1975) 56–68

Eisenstein, Zillah R. ed *Capitalist Patriarchy and the Case for Socialist Feminism* New York 1979

Firestone, Shulamith *The Dialectic of Sex* New York 1971

Gould, Carol C. 'The Woman Question: Philosophy of Liberation and the Liberation of Philosophy' in C.C. Gould and M. Wartofsky eds *Women and Philosophy* New York 1976

Guettel, Charnie *Marxism and Feminism* Toronto 1974

Harding, Sandra 'Feminism: Reform or Revolution?' in C.C. Gould and M. Wartofsky eds *Women and Philosophy* New York 1976

Held, Virginia 'Marx, Sex, and the Transformation of Society' in C.C. Gould and M. Wartofsky eds *Women and Philosophy* New York 1976

Jaggar, Alison, and Struhl, Paula eds *Feminist Frameworks* New York 1978

Kuhn, Annette, and Wolpe, Ann Marie *Feminism and Materialism: Women and Modes of Production* London 1978

Mitchell, Juliet *Women's Estate* Harmondsworth 1971

Rapp, Rayna 'Gender and Class: An Archeology of Knowledge Concerning the Origin of the State' *Dialectical Anthropology* III (1977) 309–23

Reed, Evelyn *Problems of Women's Liberation* New York 1970

Reiter, Rayna R. ed *Toward an Anthropology of Women* New York and London 1975

Rowbotham, Sheila *Women, Resistance and Revolution* Harmondsworth 1974

– *Women's Consciousness, Man's World* Harmondsworth 1973

Rubin, Gayle 'The Traffic in Women: Notes on the "Political Economy" of Sex' in R.R. Reiter ed *Toward an Anthropology of Women* New York and London 1975

Saffioti, Heleieth I.B. *Women in Class Society* tr Michael Vale with intro by Eleanor Burke Leacock, New York and London 1978

Scott, Hilda *Does Socialism Liberate Women?* Boston 1975

Smith, Dorothy 'Women and Corporate Capitalism' in Marylee Stephenson ed *Women in Canada* Don Mills 1977

Sontag, Susan 'The Third World of Woman' *Partisan Review* XL (1973) 180–206

Ursel, Jane 'The Nature and Origins of Women's Oppression: Marxism and Feminism' *Contemporary Crisis* I (1977) 23–36

THEORY AND CRITIQUE OF THEORY

Clark, Lorenne M.G. 'The Formation of the Family: Invisible Hand or Mailed Fist?' unpublished, Dept. of Philosophy, University of Toronto

- 'Politics and Law: The Theory and Practice of the Ideology of Male Supremacy' in D.N. Weisstub ed *Law and Policy* Toronto 1976; also in a slightly abridged form in J. King-Farlow and W. Shea eds *Contemporary Issues in Political Philosophy* New York 1976
- 'Privacy, Property, Freedom and the Family' in R. Bronaugh ed *Philosophical Law* Connecticut and London 1976
- 'Sexual Equality and the Problem of an Adequate Moral Theory: The Poverty of Liberalism' in 'The Search for the Feminist Perspective: The Changing Potency of Women' Special Publication No. 5 in *The Canadian Newsletter of Research on Women* Toronto 1979

Jaggar, Alison 'Political Philosophies of Women's Liberation' in M. Vetterling-Braggin, F. Ellison, and J. English eds *Feminism and Philosophy* Totowa, NJ 1977

Lange, Lynda 'Reproduction in Democratic Theory' in J. King-Farlow and W. Shea eds *Contemporary Issues in Political Philosophy* New York 1976

O'Brien, Mary 'The Dialectics of Reproduction' *International Women's Studies Quarterly* forthcoming
- 'The Politics of Impotence' in J. King-Farlow and W. Shea eds *Contemporary Issues in Political Philosophy* New York 1976
- 'The Politics of Reproduction' unpublished doctoral dissertation, York University, Toronto, 1976
- 'The Politics of Reproduction' in 'The Search for the Feminist Perspective: The Changing Potency of Women' Special Publication No. 5 in *The Canadian Newsletter of Research on Women* Toronto 1979

Okin, Susan Moller, Introduction to *Women and Citizens: Women in Western Political Thought* Princeton, forthcoming

Reiter, Rayna R. 'Unraveling the Problem of Origins: An Anthropological Search for Feminist Theory' *The Scholar and the Feminist III* Conference at Barnard College 1976 New York 1976

METAPHYSICAL AND EPISTEMOLOGICAL ISSUES

Allen, Christine Garside 'Can a Woman Be Good in the Same Way as a Man?' *Dialogue* x (1971) 534–44
- 'Sex Identity and Personal Identity' in J. King-Farlow and W. Shea eds *Values and the Quality of Life* New York 1976
- 'Women and Persons' in M. Anderson ed *Mother Was Not a Person* Montreal 1972

Code, Lorraine 'Is the Sex of the Knower Epistemologically Significant?' unpublished, Dept. of Philosophy, York University, Toronto

Marcil-Lacoste, Louise 'Féminisme et rationalité' *La rationalité aujourd'hui/Rationality Today* Ottawa, forthcoming
- 'On Repeating Men: The Case of Feminist Writings' unpublished, Département de Philosophie, Université de Montréal
Morgan, Kathryn 'Sexuality as a Metaphysical Dimension' in S. Hill and M. Weinzweig eds *Philosophical Aspects of Women's Liberation* Belmont, Calif. 1978
Payer, Mary E. 'Is Traditional Scholarship Value Free? Toward a Critical Theory' *The Scholar and the Feminist IV* Conference at Barnard College 1977 New York 1977

THE NATURE OF WOMEN

Bamberger, Joan 'The Myth of Matriarchy: Why Men Rule in Primitive Society' in M.Z. Rosaldo and L. Lamphere eds *Women, Culture and Society* Stanford 1974
Chodorow, Nancy 'Family Structure and Feminine Personality' in M.Z. Rosaldo and L. Lamphere eds *Women, Culture and Society* Stanford 1974
Dickason, Anne 'The Feminine as Universal' in M. Vetterling-Braggin, F. Elliston, and J. English eds *Feminism and Philosophy* Totawa, NJ 1977
Ehrenreich, Barbara, and English, Deirdre *For Her Own Good: 150 Years of the Experts' Advice on Women* New York 1978
Lange, Lynda 'Woman is Not a Rational Animal: On Aristotle's Biology of Reproduction' unpublished, Dept. of Philosophy, University of Toronto
Mills, Pat J. 'Women and Nature in the Frankfurt School' unpublished, Social and Political Thought, York University, Toronto
O'Faolain, Julia, and Martines, Lauro eds *Not In God's Image* Toronto 1973
Pagels, Elaine H. 'When Did Man Make God in his Image? A Case Study in Religion and Politics' *The Scholar and the Feminist III* Conference at Barnard College 1976 New York 1976
Sanday, Peggy R. 'Female Status in the Public Domain' in M.Z. Rosaldo and L. Lamphere eds *Women, Culture and Society* Stanford 1974
Trebilcot, J. 'Sex Roles: The Argument from Nature' in J. English ed *Sex Equality* Englewood Cliffs, NJ 1977
Whitbeck, Caroline 'Theories of Sex Difference' in C.C. Gould and M. Wartofsky eds *Women and Philosophy* New York 1976

THE FAMILY: MARRIAGE, SEX, AND REPRODUCTION

Benjamin, Jessica 'Authority and the Family Revisited, or, A World Without Fathers?' *New German Critique* XIII (winter 1978) 35–58

Chodorow, Nancy *The Reproduction of Mothering* Berkeley 1975

Delphy, Christine 'Continuities and Discontinuities in Marriage and Divorce' in D.L. Barker and S. Allen eds *Sexual Divisions and Society: Process and Change* London 1976

Dinnerstein, Dorothy *The Mermaid and the Minotaur* New York 1977

Hall, Diana Long 'Social Implications of the Scientific Study of Sex' *The Scholar and The Feminist IV* Conference at Barnard College 1977 New York 1977

Kelly-Gadol, Joan 'The Social Relations of the Sexes: Methodological Implications of Women's History' *Signs* I 4 (1976) 809–24

Ketchum, Sara Ann 'Liberalism and Marriage Law' in M. Vetterling-Braggin, F. Elliston, and J. English eds *Feminism and Philosophy* Totawa, NJ 1977

Leacock, Eleanor Burke, Introduction to F. Engels *The Origin of the Family, Private Property, and the State* New York 1972

Margolis, Joseph and Margolis, Clorinda 'The Separation of Marriage and the Family' in M. Vetterling-Braggin, F. Elliston, and J. English eds *Feminism and Philosophy* Totawa, NJ 1977

Oakley, Ann *Women's Work: The Housewife, Past and Present* New York 1976

O'Driscoll, Lyla H. 'On the Nature and Value of Marriage' in M. Vetterling-Braggin, F. Elliston, and J. English eds *Feminism and Philosophy* Totawa, NJ 1977

Rossi, Alice 'Maternalism, Sexuality, and the New Feminism' in J. Zubin and J. Money eds *Contemporary Sexual Behaviour* Baltimore 1972

ANDROGYNY

Allen, Christine Garside 'True Sex Polarity' unpublished, Dept. of Philosophy, Concordia University, Montreal

Ferguson, Anne 'Androgyny as an Ideal for Human Development' in M. Vetterling-Braggin, F. Elliston, and J. English eds *Feminism and Philosophy* Totawa, NJ 1977

Jaggar, Alison 'On Sexual Equality' in J. English ed *Sex Equality* Englewood Cliffs, NJ 1977

Morgan, Kathryn 'Androgyny: Vision or Mirage' unpublished, Dept. of Philosophy, University of Toronto

Trebilcot, Joyce 'Two Forms of Androgynism' in M. Vetterling-Braggin, F. Elliston, and J. English eds *Feminism and Philosophy* Totawa, NJ 1977

BOOKS AND ANTHOLOGIES

Agonito, Rosemary ed *History of Ideas on Women* New York 1977

Barker, Diana Leonard, and Allen, Sheila eds *Sexual Divisions and Society: Process and Change* London 1976

Daly, Mary *Gyn/Ecology: The Metaethics of Radical Feminism* Boston 1978

Davis, Elizabeth Gould *The First Sex* Harmondsworth 1972

De Beauvoir, Simone *The Second Sex* New York 1968

Dinnerstein, Dorothy *The Mermaid and the Minotaur* New York 1977

Eisenstein, Zillah R. ed *Capitalism, Patriarchy and the Case for Socialist Feminism* New York 1979

English, Jane ed *Sex Equality* Englewood Cliffs, NJ 1977

Figes, Eva *Patriarchal Attitudes* London 1972

Firestone, Shulamith *The Dialectic of Sex* New York 1971

Freidan, Betty *The Feminine Mystique* New York 1963

Gould, Carol C., and Wartofsky, Marx eds *Women and Philosophy: Toward a Theory of Liberation* New York 1976

Hays, H.R. *The Dangerous Sex: The Myth of Feminine Evil* New York 1964

Hill, Sharon, and Weinzweig, Marjorie eds *Philosophical Aspects of Women's Liberation* Belmont, Calif. 1978

Jaggar, Alison, and Struhl, Paula eds *Feminist Frameworks* New York 1978

King-Farlow, John, and Shea, William eds *Contemporary Issues in Political Philosophy* New York 1976

Kuhn, Annette, and Wolpe, Ann Marie *Feminism and Materialism: Women and Modes of Production* London 1978

Mahowald, Mary ed *Philosophy of Woman* Indianapolis 1978

Mitchell, Juliet *Woman's Estate* Harmondsworth 1971

Okin, Susan Moller *Women and Citizens: Women in Western Political Thought* Princeton, forthcoming

O'Neill, Onora, and Ruddick, William eds *Having Children: Philosophical and Legal Reflections on Parenthood* New York, forthcoming

Osborne, Martha Lee *Women in Western Thought* New York 1979

Reed, Evelyn *Problems of Women's Liberation* New York 1970

Reiter, Rayna R. ed *Toward an Anthropology of Women* New York and London 1975

Reuther, Rosemary R. *New Woman, New Earth* New York 1975

Rosaldo, Michelle Z., and Lamphere, Louise eds *Women, Culture and Society* Stanford 1974

Rossi, Alice S. ed *The Feminist Papers* New York 1973

Rowbotham, Sheila *Woman's Consciousness, Man's World* Harmondsworth 1973

– *Women, Resistance, and Revolution* Harmondsworth 1974

Vetterling-Braggin, Mary, Elliston, Frederick, and English, Jane eds *Feminism and Philosophy* Totawa, NJ 1977

Yates, Gayle Graham *What Women Want: The Ideas of the Movement* Cambridge, Mass. 1975